THOREAU

Thoreau

A NATURALIST'S LIBERTY

John Hildebidle

HARVARD UNIVERSITY PRESS

Cambridge, Massachusetts, and London, England

1983

Publication of this book has been aided by a grant from the
Andrew W. Mellon Foundation

Library of Congress Cataloging in Publication Data

Hildebidle, John, 1946–
Thoreau, a naturalist's liberty.

Includes index.
1. Thoreau, Henry David, 1817–1862—Knowledge—
Natural history. 2. Thoreau, Henry David, 1817–1862—
Knowledge—History. I. Title.
PS3057.N3H5 1983   818.309   82-18521
ISBN 0-674-88640-2

In memory of
Thomas McGuire
who, as I am told, taught me to walk

We would fain take that walk . . .
which is perfectly symbolical of the
path which we love to travel in the
interior and ideal world.

THOREAU

ACKNOWLEDGMENTS

THANKS ARE DUE to Joel Porte, who, when I was first investigating the peculiar American distrust of history, pointed me toward Emerson and then patiently and helpfully condoned my preference for Thoreau; to Heather McClave, who read an earlier version of this study on very short notice but with a keen critical eye; to the English Department of Harvard University, which saw fit to award that earlier version the Howard Mumford Jones Prize; to Robert Kiely, who helped convince me that it might indeed make a book; and to William Howarth, who turned my attention to the late nature essays of Thoreau, both published and unpublished.

William Hutchinson kindly offered suggestions as I struggled to learn more about natural history writing generally. Randy Fertel first pointed out to me the central importance of "Baker Farm," although he cannot be held accountable for the uses to which I have put that chapter. Many of my colleagues—among them Paul Erickson, Martin Irvine, Will Lee, Will Marquess, Daniel Penrice, Lisa Ruddick, Jack Solomon, and Nan Stone—helped immeasurably in making life both livable and educative while I was at work; and they reassured me, by their example, that one could hope to be both humane and scholarly. Elizabeth Witherell, the Editor-in-Chief, and Carolyn Kappes and Nora Mayes at the Thoreau Edition were gracious beyond all expectation in assisting my excursion south to Princeton.

Permission to quote from "Huckleberries" and from unpublished manuscript materials in the Henry W. and Albert A. Berg Collection has been granted by the New York Public Library, Astor, Lenox and Tilden Foundations.

To my fellow-saunterer Kevin Van Anglen I owe a particular debt, not only for his friendship but also for his willingness always to share both his knowledge and his wit, and each in usefully homeopathic doses.

I will not pretend to be able to record my thanks to my wife; were she not as she is, certainly this book would not be. It is my son Nicholas who gave me, throughout the rendering of this account, opportunities without number to observe that Nature is indeed mystical always.

CONTENTS

THOREAU

INTRODUCTION

IN HIS 1921 collection *The Triumph of the Egg,* Sherwood Anderson included a piece—for convenience, we may call it a story—entitled "The Man in the Brown Coat."[1] The story is the monologue, or series of monologues, of a man "sitting and writing" in his house somewhere in Iowa, "as alone as ever any man God made." What concerns him particularly is his wife. "Why," he wonders, "in all our life together, have I never been able to break through the wall to my wife?" The visible sign of his entrapment is a brown coat: "I wear a brown coat and I cannot come out of my coat. I cannot come out of myself. My wife is very gentle and she speaks softly but she cannot come out of herself."

The man in the brown coat does not, however, sit idly by; he is, by his own description, a historian: "I am writing a history of the things men do. I have written three such histories and I am but a young man. Already I have written three hundred, four hundred thousand words." That the task is a futile and even a destructive one is clear from the start. The story begins with a sample of "history" written in nursery-book prose:

> Napoleon went down into a battle riding a horse.
> Alexander went down into a battle riding on a horse.
> General Grant got off a horse and walked in a wood.
> General Hindenburg stood on a hill.
> The moon came up out of a clump of bushes.

Whether the lines are a sample of the man's writing or serve as Anderson's ironic counterpoint to the man's self-chosen task is never made

1

clear. The lines recur, slightly revised and with the addition of General
Pershing to the list of horse-borne generals, three times in a story only
a bit more than four pages long. There is no increase in the apparent
significance or insight they contain. The man is aware of his own futility; he ends the story wondering: "Why do I not say a word out of
myself to the others? Already I have written three hundred, four hundred thousand words. Are there no words that lead into life? Some day
I shall speak to myself. Some day I shall make a testament unto
myself." Despite the biblical resonance of his final vow, it is apparent
that the man in the brown coat, like so many of Anderson's "gro-
tesques," will never change, that he will continue to endure a life filled
with words no more lively than those he has already committed to
paper.

The story is short and slight, and one would not want to construct
upon or around it an elaborate scheme. But it does seem to me a fine
example, not only of certain modernist concerns, but also and more
significantly of a peculiarly American attitude toward history in particular and toward accumulated knowledge in general. The American
preference for the native, the immediate, the new, and the practical
over the European, the customary, the theoretical, and the "intellectual" has found its mythic center in the *topos* of the American Adam,
so clearly outlined by R. W. B. Lewis. The less literary, and often distinctly unpleasant, side of the same attitude has been studied by
Richard Hofstadter.[2] What is on display in Anderson's story is the
basis of this often strident rejection of the past: a very real fear of psychological and cultural suffocation by the old ways, and by the apparently endless written record of these old ways. Whether his interest in
history is the *cause* of the man in the brown coat's sad life or merely
one of its manifestations, the identification of history with emotional
and spiritual death is unequivocal.

Although the particular discipline of history is the starting point of
this study, history is not the sole focus of this fear. History, devoted as
it necessarily is to the past, is an especially obvious point of attack in a
culture committed to "making it new." Science, however, is liable to
the same charge, especially what David S. Wilson, paraphrasing
Thomas Kuhn, calls "normal science"—"plodding, continuous, responsible investigation and construction of tentative hypotheses."[3]
Science is, in very nearly the same way as history, at times the accumulation of "dead" facts. Hofstadter, for instance, points out the nearly

mythic cultural reputation of Thomas Edison, the practical inventor, and the oblivion which surrounds the career of Edison's near-contemporary Josiah Willard Gibbs, America's "greatest genius in pure science."[4] Another, and earlier, instance of the same attitude is the ridicule which James Fenimore Cooper aims at the figure of the pedantical Dr. Bat in *The Prairie*. The collection of knowledge, especially in those disciplines long honored in Europe, is simply not seen as the proper career for a true American. the results of such a life are at best comic (the foolish ramblings of Dr. Bat) and at worst, if not tragic, then at least profoundly stultifying (the impenetrable isolation of the historian in the brown coat).

And so, as R. W. B. Lewis has shown, America prefers, as an image of itself, the figure of Adam: the man without a past (and therefore without a history or any reason to be interested in history); Emerson's "simple genuine self against the whole world"; the man who is, as Lewis puts it, continuously "a figure of heroic innocence and vast potentialities, poised at the start of a new history."[5] But matters are never quite that simple. It may seem, for instance, that to be "emancipated from history, happily bereft of ancestry, untouched and undefiled by the usual inheritances of family and race . . . self-reliant and self-propelling,"[6] is an ideal, if somewhat adolescent, life. But for every Emerson welcoming the title of Adam, we can find a Hawthorne or James lamenting (if half-ironically) the absence of shadow and mystery, and more significantly of antiquity, custom, and tradition.[7] We forget, too, how dressed our naked American Adams are—Ishmael, for instance, the self-reliant loner, is after all by training and experience a member of that most culturally encumbered group, school teachers. In any case, as a twentieth-century Adam was moved to remark, "To be born unencumbered is not the complete advantage one might immediately imagine."[8]

When an American writer proclaims himself to be Adam *redivivus,* his claim is likely to arise as much from defensiveness as from self-aggrandizement.[9] Americans have long been convinced that they have no past; and characteristically, they try to turn an apparent weakness into a virtue. Norman Foerster, in a study of American nature writers published in 1923, begins with the assertion that "America is virtually without a past," and goes on to argue, as has often been done elsewhere, that what America *does* have is nature, and so it has developed a unique native literature.[10] The date of Foerster's study is significant; the book appeared almost precisely half-way between Van Wyck Brooks's "America's Coming-of-Age" (1915) and Vernon Parrington's *Main Currents in American Thought* (1927–1930)—in the midst, that is, of a major critical and literary-historical effort to find or to devise a "usable past" for American writing, an effort of which Foerster was, of course, aware.[11] This is an instance of what I take to be a fundamental paradox: America continually denies its past, and at the same time is vitally concerned with finding, inventing, and understanding that past. The resolution of the paradox is, usually, a methodological one; the problem of whether there *is* a past becomes reformulated as the question of how one may *use*, safely and productively, whatever history one may find.

I emphasize *safely;* the distrust of historical materials that lies behind this methodological search is fundamental. It is, I think, what gives rise to the paradox in the first place. "Make it new," the American modernist cries, as did his ancestors; but the phrase, apparently so confident and unequivocal, is in fact ambiguous. In one sense—the most direct sense, to be sure—it means make something which has not been made before, something unencumbered by custom, whether it be a poem, a telephone, or Emerson's much-belabored mousetrap. But at the same time, the literary works which this attitude produced— Pound's *Cantos,* for instance; or Williams' *Paterson;* or, for that matter, *Walden* and *Cape Cod*—are more often than not full of the old, of facts, personages, documents, events, and literary remains. Thus the dictum, in practice, tends to mean *re-new:* take something (or, more precisely, an array of pre-existing things and accounts) and make out of it something new. One must never admit a doubt that the new thing is necessarily (because new) better—more instructive, more real, more profound, more significant—than the old from which it is made. The early years of this century seem to have been an especially active time for writers to undertake this complex reworking of the American past—the time of Williams' *In the American Grain* and *The Great American Novel,* of Gertrude Stein's *The Making of Americans,* Paul Rosenfield's *Port of New York,* Hart Crane's *The Bridge,* Waldo Frank's *Our America* and *The Re-Discovery of America,* Gilbert Seldes' *Mainland,* and the *Cantos* in which Jefferson and Adams figure so prominently.

But it is my contention that the effort to find a safe way to use the accumulated knowledge of the past is not limited solely to the discipline of history and is not peculiarly restricted to the period of American modernism. In a recent article, James L. Machor considers five of the more important twentieth-century studies of the full range of American literature; in all five works he identifies a contradiction: "Each time they affirm that the vitality of America and its artists consists of the quest for a new world or a new myth, they discover themselves admitting that the very act is a delusive denial of history—an escapism which cashiers tradition . . . Additionally, all five find that their own desire to rediscover and recapture history has been, paradoxically, a struggle to escape history as a record of the past."[12] In my own effort to understand more fully the dynamics of this "delusive denial," I have looked backward to a writer not usually considered a historian: Henry David Thoreau. Thoreau's work provides an especially elaborated instance of the effort to make old knowledge new. He is characteristically direct in announcing his refusal to pay attention to the past and indeed to anything second-hand; yet he is, of course, equally direct in his use of an astonishing range of second-hand accounts, historical and otherwise.[13] How he manages to have it both ways at once is the concern of this study. To state the case briefly, he defines with reasonable consistency states of being in which history is of use, and states in which it is useless and even hazardous. At the same time he is careful to establish a *method* of dealing with those facts which he has not personally observed—a method which is equally efficacious in reading Lemuel Shattuck's town history of Concord or the observations of the naturalist William Bartram. The method Thoreau adopts has a name and a history of its own; it is natural history, and it is the basis not only of a science but of a body of writing which is substantial in its bulk if somewhat indefinite in its character and quality. It is my argument that Thoreau is in fact the last—and, in literary terms, overwhelmingly the most successful and important—of the natural historians.

Of course, being Thoreau, he can be labeled only partially and tentatively. I have tried to show, in the pages that follow, some of the ways in which Thoreau demonstrates his abilities as a writer of natural history, as well as some of the ways in which Thoreau turned those abilities and that method to his own unique and often quite unscientific purposes. But it is only fair to acknowledge what this study does not pretend to accomplish. I have not undertaken an evaluation of the totality of Thoreau's work—that task having already been done by Sherman Paul and, very recently, by William Howarth.[14] I would not argue that Thoreau is *only* a natural historian, and I have therefore not tried to bring within the compass of this book those works in which Thoreau's most pressing interest is, for example, politics. I am most interested in natural history as a literary method and indeed as a literary *genre;* I have, as a consequence, put aside the question of the accuracy of Thoreau's science. The continuing and admirable labor of the Princeton Edition will in time no doubt resolve for us whether "The Succession of Forest Trees" propounds an accurate scientific hypothesis; for my purposes it is enough to observe that in his lecture Thoreau intended to be a careful scientist, whether or not he succeeded.

Finally, I would insist on what any informed reader of Thoreau will find obvious in the chapters that follow: that, however central natural history as a method of observation and as a method of writing is to Thoreau, it is only one element of the rich complexity of his accomplishment. My reading of *Walden,* for instance, is selective and partial—as I believe any reading of that book must be. I would only hope that the limitations of my approach are, in the end, productive, and that they will allow Thoreau to be read, or reread, with greater appreciation. Randall Jarrell writes somewhere of the peculiarity of so many critical studies, which stand, as he puts it, in relation to reader and text as the wall did to Pyramus and Thisbe. I would not necessarily presume I have altogether avoided that obstructive role; but I would offer instead the image of the knothole through which Thoreau peered on his excursion to Cape Cod and which yielded "the long-wished-for insight," hoping that it may be said of this study that "though to him that knocketh it may not always be opened, yet to him that looketh long enough through a knot-hole the inside shall be visible" (*Cape Cod,* 77).*

---

*Full bibliographic information on Thoreau's works will be found in the Abbreviations of Sources.

PRESENTING
THE PAST:
THOREAU
AND
HISTORY

Aᴎᴀʟʏsᴛs of Thoreau's remarks on history have generally taken them rather too literally.[1] It must of course be admitted that Thoreau seems, especially in *A Week on the Concord and Merrimack Rivers,* unequivocal in his denial of the validity of history. "The *past,*" he announces, "cannot be *presented*" (*Week,* 155), apparently settling the issue, as he not infrequently does, by wordplay. In his late essay "Walking," he makes the same argument in a slightly different way: "Above all, we cannot afford not to live in the present. He is blessed over all mortals who loses no moment of the passing life in remembering the past." (*Excursions,* 245–246). But a careful reader of Thoreau must learn to distrust the epigrammatic force of many of his most well-known and clearly stated dicta. Thoreau, devoted as he was to the reading of antiquarian history and travel books and to the writing of careful accounts of the past, cannot, by his own definition, be said to be blessed.

Sherman Paul argues that Thoreau used the fruits of his reading "to prove the indifference of time and place."[2] That is certainly often true, but such a conclusion simplifies the case in exactly the way in which Thoreau himself was prone to simplify it. In trying to resolve the knotty question of what to do with and about history, and indeed with and about the accumulating bulk of remembered knowledge generally, Thoreau seems driven to supplant ambiguity with epigram. Paul acknowledges, of course, that we cannot take Thoreau's apparent rejection of history quite at face value: "He was not so unmindful of history as one might assume from his views of the past. For the issue was not, as has often been supposed, a repudiation of all history, but rather a refusal to serve the authority of the past."[3] It is toward a better understanding of how Thoreau intended to escape this service, while at the same time allowing himself the use of historical material and of historical methods, that this chapter is aimed. A convenient place to begin is *A Week,* Thoreau's first extended work.

The book is, as explicitly as is *Walden,* a remembrance; even, I am tempted to say, a history. Certainly it uses historical materials and sources of the most traditional sort; we have not reached the bottom of the first page before we find Thoreau quoting "the historian of Concord," Lemuel Shattuck, with the wry introduction "I love to quote so good authority" (*Week,* 5). A few pages later Thoreau cites, at length, Johnson's *Wonder-Working Providence* (pp. 10–11); and Channing's annotations identify references to John Smith's *A Description of New England,* Raleigh's *History of the World,* and, repeatedly, Fox's *History of Dunstable.* Thoreau himself identifies another source, "Belknap, the historian of New Hampshire" (p. 123).

It is worth noting that in *A Week* Thoreau does not seem at all critical of his sources, in the way, for instance, that he is critical of the authority of maps and atlases in "Chesuncook" — each reference there being accompanied by the observation that the maps are wrong (*Maine Woods,* 86, 94, 153). But it is not merely a question of quotation of authorities. *A Week* is certainly more than what H. S. Canby called it: "an anthology carried upon a frame of story."[4] Rather, it is a record of a journey backward in time, as Lawrence Buell demonstrates, and, if we are to believe Buell, an attempt to "take in the whole cultural history of mankind."[5] Certainly it is a *personal* history of an actual event which was, by the time the book came to be written, well past;[6] and indeed, as it stands, it is a series of memoirs contained within a memoir. In the course of "Monday" Thoreau finds occasion to recall an earlier excursion up the Nashua; and the central event of "Tuesday," and one of the central events of the book as a whole, is a reminiscence of Thoreau's earlier and solitary hike up Mt. Greylock.

One effect of these intrusions of the more distant past is to interrupt the progress of what Buell would have us take as a regular "movement backward in time toward an ideal, Arcadian world."[7] Indeed, the Nashua incident (*Week,* 162–166) seems to be intended to confuse any sort of clear progression or regression in time. Apparently provoked by the two brothers' passing of the junction of the Merrimack and Nashua rivers, it is introduced in a way that explicitly emphasizes the jump in space and time: "Far away from here, in Lancaster, with another companion, I have crossed the broad valley of the Nashua, over which we had so long looked westward from the Concord hills without seeing it to the blue mountains in the horizon." The reminiscence immediately drives Thoreau even further back chronologically, to the period when, looking from Concord, he had overlooked the valley entirely. Recalling the earlier trip gives Thoreau another angle of vision; for the previous journey includes a moment spent looking from a hill that is now "yonder . . . on the road to Tyngsboro," a view which includes, in its turn, exactly the place where Thoreau and his brother are.

The confusions of time and space, the triple points of view, are not resolved; we are told almost nothing *about* the earlier trip, except that it happened and that it had an intriguingly magical quality, that it was a trip to the "Delectable Mountains" like that undertaken by "Rasselas and other inhabitants of happy valleys." The account—or rather, the nonaccount—concludes with the recognition that this particular excursion has recurred repeatedly, not only "in imagination" as at the present moment, but literally: "We have since made many similar excursions to the principal mountains of New England and New York, and even far in the wilderness, and have passed a night on the summit of many of them." The "we" is significant. Usually in *A Week* the "we" indicates Henry and John. Here, it seems, the "we" is either more general or editorial, since the earlier trip was with "another companion" and since John has, by the time the book is written, tragically died (an event implicit in much of the mood of the book, if never explicitly acknowledged) and yet: "now, when we look again westward from our native hills, Wachusett and Monadnock have retreated once more among the blue and fabulous mountains in the horizon, though our eyes rest on the very rocks on both of them, where we have pitched our tent for a night, and boiled our hasty-pudding." "We" are back where we started, except of course that "we" is now singular. That change underscores the point that the circularity is only geographical, the repetition only partial; time will not, except when it is transformed into language, allow itself to be so bent that it may repeat itself in every detail. And even then, the repetition is, at bottom, only a matter of words, not facts.[8]

In one sense, this is Thoreau using the past to defeat itself; or rather, using the written record of the past—its *history*—to defeat the normal limitations of space and time. The same device is used in a more direct and compressed form in the "Ktaadn" section of *The Maine Woods,* where the movement in space toward and then up Mt. Ktaadn serves as the vehicle for a movement in language and reference which in turn allows Thoreau to move backward through time to the world of "Chaos and ancient Night" (*Maine Woods,* 60 and 64). Three times in the course of his ascent of the mountain Thoreau invokes the name and example of Satan and his journey in Book II of *Paradise Lost.* Thoreau's Pisgah vision from the summit is of nature before and without man:

> It is difficult to conceive of a region uninhabited by man . . . And yet we have not seen pure Nature, unless we have seen her thus vast, and drear, and inhuman . . . This was that Earth of which we have heard, made out of Chaos and Old Night. Here was no man's garden, but the unhandselled globe. It was not lawn, nor pasture, nor mead, nor woodland, nor lea, nor arable, nor waste-land. It was the fresh and natural surface of the planet Earth, as it was made forever and ever, — to be the dwelling of man, we say, — so Nature made it, and man may use it if he can. Man was not to be associated with it.   (*Maine Woods,* 70)

"So Nature made it" — this is Genesis without God. The choice of Satan over Adam is not merely perversity or a stab at originality; it is essential, at this extreme of return to the primitive. Thoreau has managed to go back to a primeval prehuman timelessness, to the Eden of the eternal present and eternally wild, an Eden that is no garden and therefore, by its very nature, an Eden that can have no Adam.[9] To someone who desires to live in the present, this is one possible justification of fronting the past; pursued far enough, the past destroys itself.

But *A Week* does not go this far, nor is the Earth of Chaos and Old Night a place that will allow Thoreau or any man to settle; indeed Thoreau's very presence there is a denial of its fundamental nature, which is not to be "associated with" man in any way, even, we suspect, with man as spectator. The climbing of Ktaadn represents one extreme, both in Thoreau's effort to work his way backward, imaginatively, in time, and in his recurrent consideration of the question of what to do with that child of time, history. *A Week* is, as its form and manner might suggest, a much less decisive work in these regards; indeed its value for my present purpose lies in the range of opinions it contains.

I skipped rather quickly over the point that the action of *A Week* occurs at a time considerably prior to the time of its final reconstruction into book form. On its face, this is hardly an important observation, especially regarding a work of Romantic autobiography built around the exercise of memory. Despite the Transcendental fondness for journal-writing, the effort to keep writing rigorously in the present had to wait until the craze for automatic writing, until Dada and "improvisation" such as *Kora in Hell.* But as a record of the past, *A Week,* as we have already noticed, is a violation of Thoreau's confident dictum in "Walking"; and the violation is made all the more obvious by the precision with which the excursion is dated: "At length, on Saturday, the last day of August, 1839, we two, brothers, and natives of Concord, weighed anchor in this river port" (*Week,* 16). There is an apparent similarity, on the point of placing the events so unequivocally in the past, between this and (for example) "Tintern Abbey" ("Five years have passed . . .") and to the beginnings of "A Yankee in Canada," *Cape Cod,* and each of the parts of *The Maine Woods.* But with due allowance having been made for a main current of Romanticism, and for an apparent stylistic habit of Thoreau's, the dating of *A Week* has some particular significance. It is not, after all, as though Thoreau felt constrained by the facts of the matter; he unblushingly compresses the two weeks of the actual trip into one literary week. But the date of the voyage is not simply a fact; it is a fact at the opposite side, chronologically, of an even greater fact: the death of John Thoreau. That sad event is what makes the "pastness" of the excursion especially important, and especially irredeemable, and lends the work that elegiac mood to be found, among other places, in Thoreau's poem to an unnamed "maiden" and, implicitly, to John (*Week,* 47–48):

> Still will I strive to be
> As if thou wert with me;
> Whatever path I take,
> It shall be for thy sake,
> Of gentle slope and wide,
> As thou wert by my side,
> Without a root
> To trip thy gentle foot.

The same note appears in Thoreau's consideration of those myths about "promising youths who have died a premature death" (p. 58) and in the moving portion of the long essay on friendship where Thoreau wonders how to say good-bye: "Have you any *last* words? Alas, it is only the word of words, which you have so long sought and found not; *you* have not a *first* word yet" (p. 273). Insofar as *A Week* is elegiac, in a broad if not a strictly technical sense, the fact that the past cannot be presented, far from being an aesthetic and philosophical virtue, is a source of pain; nor can that past so confidently be repudiated and its record discarded as irrelevant.

ONE NEED NOT, of course, rely entirely on implicit evidence. *A Week* contains a considerable amount of explicit discussion of the value of history and how it should be written and read. It is unrealistic to hope that the cumulative effect of these direct comments will show a clear and unwavering position, but they can be used to lay out the terms and the range of Thoreau's thinking on the subject.

On the one hand, Thoreau equates history with mere waste: "It is easier to discover another such new world as Columbus did, than to go within one fold of this which we appear to know so well; the land is lost sight of, the compass varies, and mankind mutiny; and still history accumulates like rubbish before the portals of nature" (p. 383). The point here is, of course, larger than a mere attack on history; it is at the same time a criticism of the way we customarily look at nature — from our usual poor vantage point, only at her portals — and, more important, of the way we convince ourselves that we are seeing well when we are not. Still, history is, in the present instance, the specific target; and the first complaint against it is that it is simply unimportant: "Most revolutions in society have not power to interest; still less alarm us; but tell me that our rivers are drying up, or the genus pine dying out in the country, and I might attend. Most events recorded in history are more remarkable than important, like eclipses of the sun and moon, by which all are attracted, but whose effects no one takes the trouble to calculate" (p. 129). This explicit preference for natural history over the human variety is, as I will argue shortly, fundamental in Thoreau's view of things; but the passage is not quite so forthright as it seems, at least to a modern reader. To be sure, in an age that has gone beyond the superstition that the sky is full of demons, eclipses seem more remarkable than important. But is the fact that no one takes the trouble to calculate the effects of those events a critique of the events themselves (which are not *without* effects) or of

the inadequacies of the observers? Is the problem with history the ir-
relevance of the events it records? Or is the inadequacy of the historical
record of those events (which indeed often prefers the remarkable over
the important) due to faulty understanding of the events? Or is it the
reader who distorts? In short, the puzzling question remains: who is
the villain—history, the historian, or the reader of histories?

Certainly part of the difficulty Thoreau finds with history as we
have it is that, far from being only remarkable rubbish, it has the
"effect" of being an ominous burden: "Men execute nothing so
faithfully as the wills of the dead, to the last codicil and letter. *They*
rule this world, and the living are but their executors . . . Or rather,
like some Indian tribes, we bear about with us the mouldering relics of
our ancestors on our shoulders . . . All men are partially buried in the
grave of custom, and of some we see only the crown of the head above
ground. Better are the physically dead, for they more lively rot"
(*Week*, 131–132). Thoreau here is careful not to blame history, but
men; they are the ones who execute the wills, who bear the mouldering relics. The rejection of history itself, of the accumulation of
custom and tradition which the record of the past serves to codify,
might be salutary in disinterring the living; but it would be a case of
mistaking the symptom for the disease.

The question then is not how to discard history but how to read it
aright. In the first place, Thoreau insists on the primacy, not of the
record, but of the reader: "I should say that the useful results of science
had accumulated, but that there had been no accumulation of knowledge, strictly speaking, for posterity; for knowledge is to be acquired
only by a corresponding experience. How can we *know* what we are
told merely? Each man can interpret another's experience only by his
own" (p. 365; and cf. p. 155). So accumulation can be redeemed by
correspondence. The effect of this kind of reading can be very nearly
magical: "All events which make the annals of the nations are but the
shadows of our private experiences. Suddenly and silently the eras
which we call history awake and glimmer in us, and *there* is room for
Alexander and Hannibal to march and conquer. In short, the history
which we read is only a fainter memory of events which have happened in our own experience. Tradition is a more interrupted and
feebler memory" (p. 292). This prescription is a partial contradiction
of Thoreau's insistence on the active and individual role of the reader.
It seems that, at a crucial point, the effective agency shifts from the

reader to the text, which begins to awake and glimmer *in* us. We are the location of the action but not necessarily the actors.

The influence of Emerson is apparent here, and may help clarify the problem of agency. In one of the most familiar passages in "History," Emerson argues that "All history becomes subjective; in other words there is properly no History, only Biography. Every mind must know the whole lesson for itself—must go over the whole ground. What it does not see, what it does not live, it will not know. What the former age has epitomized into a formula or rule for manipular convenience, it will lose all the good of verifying for itself, by means of the wall of that rule."[10] And earlier in the same essay Emerson insists, as Thoreau does, on the standard of correspondence: "The world exists for the education of each man. There is no age or state of society or model of action in history, to which there is not somewhat corresponding in his life."[11] The difference between the two men—which, at this point, is small—seems to lie in the relative subjectivity of the observer. Emerson argues that "Of the universal mind each individual man is one more incarnation. All its properties consist in him. Each new fact in his private experience flashes a light on what great bodies of men have done, and the crises of his life refer to national crises."[12] Thoreau, of course, would not object to the idea that the microcosm (man) incarnates or recapitulates the macrocosm (history, the universal mind); else why lavish so much effort on measuring one small pond? But he is slightly more convinced of the importance of the outside, the other, the fact, if you will, upon which Emerson claims the "light" of "private experience" flashes. In Thoreau, the direction of the light, at least metaphorically, is *from* the fact *to* the individual:

> Of what moment are facts that can be lost,—which need to be commemorated? The monument of death will outlast the memory of the dead. The pyramids do not tell the tale which was confided to them; the living fact commemorates itself. Why look in the dark for light? Strictly speaking, the historical societies have not recovered one fact from oblivion . . . The fathers of history were not anxious to preserve, but to learn the fact; and hence it was not forgotten. Critical acumen is exerted in vain to uncover the past; the *past* cannot be *presented;* we cannot know what we are not. But one veil hangs over past, present, and future, and it is the province of the historian to find out, not what was but what is. (*Week,* 154–155)

If that discovery is the task of the historian, the question remains how he is to accomplish it. The model Emerson prefers, both for the reading and (to judge from *Representative Men*) for the writing of history, is biography; and indeed biography moving toward mythography. Thoreau insists that the true or useful history must be exaggerated; in his essay on Carlyle, he had said: "Exaggerated history is poetry, and truth referred to a new standard. To a small man every greater is an exaggeration. He who cannot exaggerate is not qualified to utter truth" (*Early Essays*, 264–265). The particular kind of exaggeration he prefers in *A Week* is myth: "To some extent, mythology is only the most ancient history and biography . . . The poet is he who can write some pure mythology to-day without the aid of posterity . . . We moderns . . . collect only the raw materials of biography and history, 'memoirs to serve for a history,' which itself is but the materials to serve for a mythology" (p. 60). He goes on to invoke the example of one of his own favorite myths (Columbus) and another, which a later period will find less compelling (Franklin). The quiet and automatic equation of history and biography is Emersonian; the placing of both at the same level of truth, and indeed the suggestion that there may be a hierarchy in which biography is lowest, sets Thoreau a bit apart from the Emerson of "History." We should not too quickly dismiss the task of collecting raw materials; it *is* better than accumulating rubbish. Thoreau places it on a low moral and philosophical plane; but still "collecting" is, in science if not in history, the activity to which he devoted himself more and more—we should recall his long walks with a heavy book for pressing leaves and the notched stick for taking measurements; and the pages of "raw materials" in the later journals.

The gain in moving from fact to myth, from raw material to exaggeration, is accompanied by a loss, a point which Thoreau made in discussing Carlyle's style. As a writer, and a serious one, he was continuously aware of the limitations of writing: "What a drop in the bucket is the printed word. Feeling, thought, speech, writing, and we might add poetry, inspiration—for so the circle is completed; how they gradually dwindle at length, passing through successive colanders, into your history and classics, from the roar of the ocean, the murmur of the forest, to the squeak of a mouse; so much only passed and spelt out, and punctuated, at last" (*Early Essays*, 228). The particular issue of how and whether to write history begins to merge into the larger question of how and whether to write at all, how to find and use an appropriate and effective language to say, generally and publicly, what needs to be said. On the narrower issue, the point to be made here is that what Thoreau can find is not (despite the often assertive *manner* of his prose) equations and dicta, but something more like dynamic approximations. If exaggeration, in the direction of myth, is an ideal, it is an ideal with a built-in hazard: exaggeration, and indeed any application of language to fact, contains within itself the possibility of dilution and loss. Saints—heroes, poets, truth-tellers—may need to exaggerate; lesser mortals might better stick to the facts.

In his description of the "circle" in this early essay, Thoreau seems to have left out what we might expect as the first step: "Feeling, thought, speech, writing . . . inspiration." Where, one wonders, is observation? I suspect that at a somewhat later period Thoreau would have put more emphasis on the primacy, in time and to some degree in importance, of careful *seeing*. The model Thoreau has for the only useful and true approach to history is that of the observer, the natural historian. It is a connection he makes explicit in an early journal entry: "Properly speaking, there can be no history but natural history" (*Journal*, I, 325: 8 March 1842).

The phrase immediately strikes one as a pun, and might have appealed to Thoreau on that basis alone. But the association is more than purely verbal; or rather, the confusion of language between history and natural history is very near the center of Thoreau's, as of Emerson's, consideration of the problem. One could go through Emerson's "History" simply noting the lexical changes rung on the title, in a way Thoreau may have had in mind when he set to work constructing his own "Economy." To apply the term "fact" to the past is to approach the verbal question head on; is the fact the event, the record, or the remembrance? That is, is history simply the past itself, whether remembered or (as most of it is) unremembered and thus unrecoverable? Or is it the written record, the selection from (and exaggeration of, for good or ill) the nearly infinite sequence of human and natural events that have occurred, up to the very last moment? Or is the term *history* to be taken as a kind of shorthand for the accumulation of custom and habit which is based in the past and buttressed by the (miswritten and misread) histories which too many students, in school and out, have at hand? The answer is, all three, and almost interchangeably. The intersection of the three, the crucial point, is more often clouded than distinguished by Emerson's and Thoreau's use of the word.

THERE IS a moment near the end of "A Yankee in Canada" which can serve as a convenient, and conveniently ambiguous, emblem both of this confusion of language and of the problems that lie behind it.

In his visit to Quebec City, Thoreau is particularly struck by the fortifications of the citadel. They afford him the opportunity for one of his worst puns, involving a prowling cat, a loophole, and "*mus-catry*" (*Excursions,* 73). More significantly, they allow him to define what is *wrong* about Canada, beyond its simply being Catholic, French, and not Massachusetts. The fort is a physical result and a physical representation of that weight of misapplied custom which has set Canada on the wrong course: "Those who first built this fort, coming from Old France with the memory and tradition of feudal days and customs weighing on them, were unquestionably behind their age; and those who now inhabit and repair it are all behind their ancestors or predecessors. Those old chevaliers thought they could transplant the feudal system to America. It has been set out, but it has not thriven" (*Excursions,* 81). Emerson, in "History," had argued with reference to "the Greek genius" that architecture is at least as valuable as "civil history" and literature as "sources of information."[13] Thoreau here seems to apply the method to Canada. And we have in this case a look backward by the Quebecois which, unlike Thoreau's in *A Week* or on Ktaadn, is harmful—perhaps because the look does not go back far enough, or perhaps because, while looking backward, the Quebecois have allowed themselves to be tricked into trying to live backward.

Having established at great length the connection between his travelogue and his interpretation of the culture, Thoreau in the succeeding chapter returns to the citadel, now in the hope of seeing the surrounding landscape. The temptation to indulge in wordplay, this time borrowed, is irresistible; he cites the legend of Cartier's pilot naming the place by exclaiming "in Norman French, 'Que bec!, (What a beak!)." And he cannot overlook the irony that it is only from the walls of the fortress, "and not from a solitary and majestic river cape alone, that this view is obtained." All this is by way of prologue; having laid out the necessary ground, he speaks of the view itself:

> I associate the beauty of Quebec with the steel-like and flashing air, which may be peculiar to that season of the year, in which the blue flowers of the succory and some late goldenrods and buttercups on the summit of Cape Diamond were almost my only companions, — the former bluer than the heavens they faced. Yet even I yielded in some

degree to the influence of historical associations, and found it hard to
attend to the geology of Cape Diamond or the botany of the Plains of
Abraham . . . You look out from the ramparts of the citadel beyond
the frontiers of civilization . . . Thus the citadel under my feet and all
historical associations, were swept away again by an influence from the
wilds and from Nature, as if the beholder had read her history, — an
influence which, like the Great River itself, flowed from the Arctic
fastnesses and Western forests with irresistible tide over all. (*Excursions*, 88–89)

The writing in this passage moves in a course parallel to the explicit
point; for instance, Thoreau yields to historical associations in his language before he makes the point directly, by finding the air as "steel-like and flashing" as the swords which were once employed on these
walls. The conflict between historical associations — the dead hand of
the past, if you will — and the immediate and natural is clear; so is the
exemplary difficulty which even hard-headed Thoreau has in keeping
his priorities clear ("I . . . found it hard to attend to geology"). Yet
the task of attending, however difficult, is not impossible. The bulk of
observed detail in the passage, somewhat abbreviated by my elisions,
makes it clear that the natural and the present constitute the real object; or rather the real vehicle. The advantage of this place, even if one
must risk historical associations and French cooking, and must literally
stand on the past to see the view, is that one can, as at the top of
Ktaadn, look beyond or behind time — "beyond the frontiers of
civilization." Of course Thoreau chooses to look predominantly west
(the furthest point he can see is "further west, the distant Val
Cartier"), as, in "Walking," he announces that his compass always
settles westerly. In the end, the moment, as he must have hoped, is a
transcendent one, with everything, including all historical associations, swept away — a smaller and North American analogue to that
quintessential Romantic moment when Wordsworth reaches the summit of Snowden.

But the moment of transcendence contains a surprise of exactly the
verbal sort we should expect: history is swept away, to be replaced by
a clear view of . . . history. One should not be overclever; as Stanley
Cavell says in discussing *Walden*, Thoreau means what he says, and
here he is clearly saying that history gives way before nature. But
Cavell's precise argument is that Thoreau "means every word [he]
says."[14] It is a fair enough point, but one which gets us back into

trouble here, because the word Thoreau chooses to associate with that "influence from the wilds and from Nature" is *history*. We must assume that he does not mean either *Wonder-Working Providence* or rubbish.

If he means, as seems likely, what we and he customarily call natural history, the passage is echoed often elsewhere. Near the end of *A Week* he experiences a similar moment: "While I sit here listening to the waves which ripple and break on this shore, I am absolved from all obligation to the past, and the council of nations may reconsider its vote" (p. 359). The first great advantage of natural history over other histories is precisely that it does not include an "obligation to the past." But the term *natural history* needs to be stretched beyond its most particular and customary meaning. Emerson wrote of the natural history of the intellect, not a subject we usually find in our curricula, at least under that name; and Thoreau finds occasion to speak of the "whole history of commerce" in a way which makes it sound, at least in method, more like the kind of observation we think of as natural history than like the investigation of Dr. Dryasdust.

Thoreau makes this observation when he is on his river voyage and, having just passed "the humble village of Litchfield," notices a scow being mended on the bank of the Merrimack (*Week*, 216–217).[15] Suddenly it occurs to him that "the whole history of commerce [is] made manifest in that scow turned bottom upward on the shore." As elsewhere, the irony is that the accidental and unwritten records prove, in Thoreau's mind, to be better than the intentional and written ones. By seeing the scow and the carpenters, and by looking at them with an intelligent eye, Thoreau can understand an elaborate historical and cultural process. Not that the written records are useless; he cites "The Adventures of Henry the fur-trader," Ovid, and Xenophon's *Anabasis* to support his point. But the written sources— and an odd lot they are! — are supplemental rather than fundamental; the effective reader of history, in this case, is one who observes the present carefully. It is this application of the methods of the natural historian to the task usually assigned to the ordinary historian that Thoreau seems to believe will work; the result then is not history discarded but history well read: "We should read history as little critically as we consider landscape" (*Week*, 154).

We might pause to define what such reading will involve. What the natural historian must do is, first, observe carefully and clearly; then describe, again with precision, without lapsing into connotation or association. That description will involve both accurate naming and careful cataloging; that is, defining both the uniqueness of the thing observed, and its place in larger categories and relations. The birth of natural history as a serious, widespread, and commonly accepted endeavor in the eighteenth century was fundamentally a matter of *classification;* and the fundamental sense in that endeavor was sight. Linnaeus, greatest of the early naturalists, defined the naturalist as one who "distinguishes the parts of natural bodies with his eyes, describes them appropriately according to their number, form, position, and proportion, and he names them."[16]

That the task of looking, describing, and naming is very close indeed to the heart of what Thoreau attempted, again and again, to do, seems clear enough. But the idea of Thoreau as naturalist has been a troublesome one. Thoreau's biographer, H. S. Canby, in attempting to categorize Thoreau as a scientist, calls him a "classificationist"—a name which once held much more honor than it does to modern ears. Canby is trying to redeem Thoreau from the image of *mere* naturalist—that is, as an eccentric observer of birds, with little seriousness as a writer or thinker: "The truth was that he would look close enough to learn more, but not too close lest his vision be lost. No scientist is made this way. Even as a classificationist and even in botany, Thoreau was beaten from the start. His laborious experiments, which got him nowhere because they were under no effective control, are pathetic."[17] One is tempted to ask whether all his laborious experiments—say, measuring Walden Pond—were pathetic. But the description of what Thoreau did, if not the judgment of its value and outcome, appears to be correct. And it is a fair summary of what Thoreau *said* he wanted to do, although it would seem he had something more rigorous in mind when he made the compilations of data in the late journals. In *A Week,* for instance, just before the sentence cited above ("While I sit here listening to the waves . . ."), he makes an explicitly unclassificationist assertion: "If we see the reality in things, of what moment is the superficial and apparent longer? What are the earth and all its interests beside the deep surmise which pierces and scatters them?" (p. 359). There are sciences, and scientists, who can afford to ignore the apparent for the deep surmise; but not the naturalist, not the classificationist. He must work the other way, to see as clearly as he can those elements of the apparent which serve to identify and define. And if we go back to Thoreau's statement about reading history as we read landscape, we notice another verbal surprise: "We should read history as *little* critically as we consider the landscape" (my italics). Elsewhere Thoreau emphasizes the *activity* of the reader; we might expect him to extoll that kind of active and thoughtful reading which we usually call critical, as an antidote to weak or inadequate vision. But instead he asks for a view from the middle distance, a kind of impressionism that seems ill-suited to a scientist:

> We should read history as little critically as we consider the landscape, and be more interested by the atmospheric tints and various lights and shades which the intervening spaces create, than by its groundwork and composition. It is the morning now turned evening and seen in the west, — the same sun, but a new light and atmosphere. Its beauty is like the sunset, not a fresco painting on a wall, flat and bounded, but atmospheric and roving or free. In reality, history fluctuates as the face of a landscape from morning to evening. What is of moment is its hue and color. Time hides no treasures; we want not its then but its now. (p. 154)

To call this impressionism is not necessarily to imply carelessness; the observation is careful, but *what* we are to look for and at is defined in an unexpected way. Unexpected, that is, if we compare Thoreau, as Canby does, with Agassiz rather than with Wordsworth; for we could parallel this definition of proper reading, of true sight, with passages in *The Prelude.* Wordsworth, like Thoreau, would not have us ignore the actual; halfway up Snowden he saw a hedgehog, and so he tells us he saw it, to make it clear that this is a real mountain and a real climb before (at least chronologically) it is a visionary place. But one message of *The Prelude,* to oversimplify radically, is that the eye, while essential, is not finally reliable; and that it is most effective at a certain distance, so that the distortions of the "microscopic view" are avoided.[18] Thoreau's way of putting it shares Wordsworth's implication of the limitations of science: "But, after all, it is much easier to discover than to see when the cover is off. It has been well said that 'the attitude of inspection is prone.' Wisdom does not inspect, but behold. We must look a long time before we can see . . . We do not learn by inference and deduction and the application of mathematics to philosophy, but by direct intercourse and sympathy" (*Excursions,* 131). This is from that most peculiar book review, "The Natural History of Massachusetts." The passage, with its proliferation of verbs of seeing in an effort to work around to the right one for the particular kind of sensuous response Thoreau wants, has its roots in Emerson's *Nature.* "Wisdom does not inspect, but behold" — wisdom, that is, does not number and classify but prefers to look form a certain elevation and at a certain distance, not so far that details are lost utterly, but far enough so that the combination or interrelation of details may be seen clearly, and one may see, if one is fortunate, not only the river at Quebec or the landscape near Snowden, but "the emblem of a mind . . ./In sense conducting to ideal from,/In soul of more than mortal privilege."[19] Emerson had said that the goal was to look at facts as symbols.[20] "We need pray," Thoreau says in *A Week,* "for no higher heaven than the pure senses can furnish, a *purely* sensuous life. Our present senses are but the rudiments of what they are destined to become . . . The eyes were not made for such grovelling uses as they are now put to and worn out by, but to behold beauty now invisible" (p. 382).

BOTH Wordsworth and Thoreau have taken us back to heaven, back among the saints. That serves well as an ideal but will not be very helpful for the quotidian; and the mere mortal, trapped in the day-by-day, could, in Thoreau's view of things, do considerably worse than be an accumulator of the facts of natural history: "we will not complain of the pioneer, if he raises no flowers with his first crop. Let us not underrate the value of a fact; it will one day flower in a truth. It is astonishing how few facts of importance are added in a century to the natural history of any animal. The natural history of man himself is still being gradually written" (*Excursions,* 130). Lacking a universally effective method of *making* facts (historical or otherwise) flower into truth, Thoreau falls back on the faith that the flower will appear someday, to someone. How it will happen, is less certain; it is not clear whether the flowering will be the action of the fact (as the metaphor suggests) or of the observer, the "true man of science [who] will know nature better by his finer organization; he will smell, taste, see, hear, feel better than other men" (p. 131). If one cannot always feel oneself to be a giant, how reassuring still to be sure there *are* giants; it is a faith that has its roots in that breed of Romanticism which can at least remember the days when we trailed clouds of glory, and can record the *fact* if not always recreate the *process* of attaining that state.

And it is a faith that allows Thoreau, when sainthood is not upon him, to work diligently at the pioneering task of being a natural historian.

· 2 ·

CIRCUMSTANCES
LAID TOGETHER:
THE METHOD
OF THE
NATURAL
HISTORIAN

To UNDERSTAND more completely how Thoreau stands in relation to the more customary natural historians, we need now to expand and to investigate the definition I offered, a few pages ago, of the task and method of the natural historian. For this purpose, I will use as examples two of the most popular works of natural history ever written in English, both known to Thoreau: Gilbert White's *Natural History of Selborne* and Charles Darwin's *The Voyage of the Beagle*. That these are only examples should be clear from the beginning; the same task might well be undertaken using other works, books that may have had a more specific and explicit influence on Thoreau's writing. But since I wish to see Thoreau in the light of a method and genre of writing, and not in the light of specific works or writers, I use White and Darwin. And, as I hope will become apparent, there are appealing reasons for the choice.

The question, then, is what precisely *is* natural history, as it has usually been written? David E. Allen has remarked on the "convenient vagueness" of the term,[1] and I would not pretend that naturalism as a field of endeavor or as a kind of writing is easily definable. I will, in time, argue that this very vagueness may have drawn Thoreau to natural history as a literary field. What is important now is to recognize that too many judgments of Thoreau's writing as science or natural history have been based on artificially clear distinctions. Here, for instance, is H. S. Canby, again attempting to summarize Thoreau's failings as a scientist: "Thus [Thoreau's] objective was literary, philosophic, not really scientific. Even as geography, Thoreau's science is always amateur. It is the science of the self-made student who labors excessively for small returns because he lacks frames of reference and good methods. And in Thoreau's case it remained amateur because he was really more interested in the literature to be made of it than in the facts themselves."[2] The last sentence is surely correct, but hangs on a distinction which distorts what Thoreau was attempting—the distinction between literature and fact. Indeed, Canby's whole judgment relies on categories ill suited to the case of a writer who died in 1862—between "philosophic" and "scientific" for instance (a differentiation in terms that was not entirely clear at the time), and between professional and amateur.

The career of Darwin is a case in point. It is not certain at what stage he stopped being the gentleman-observer, of somewhat erratic training, who sailed on the *Beagle*. He refers to himself, in his 1845 Preface to the journal of his voyage,[3] as filling the position of "some scientific person," but his apparent preference is for the less rigorous term "naturalist."[4] Viewing his career as a whole, we must concede to Darwin the title "scientist." But the idea that the self-made student can be categorically set apart from the professional scientist simply will not hold.[5] There were men who devoted their lives to science—Agassiz and Asa Gray, for instance. But more often than not (and necessarily, given the state of scientific education) such men were self-made—Lyell, for instance, was a lawyer; Gilbert White's beloved John Ray, a classicist and Hebraicist; the great German traveler Humboldt, a civil servant and mining engineer.[6]

More to the point, perhaps, is the issue of "good methods." I have tried to suggest that Thoreau, with full knowledge, applies the methods of natural history to the reading and writing of history generally. What I propose to do now is to consider briefly what those methods are, as Thoreau might have known them; and to point to the ways in which he *intentionally* altered them. As will be apparent, I hope, we must abandon the modern notion of a fixed and rigorous scientific method. In the end, Canby is right. Thoreau, however interested he was in naturalism, was by no absolute standard a scientist, nor was he, by choice, simply a natural historian. However, the appropriate distinction between Thoreau and the tradition of amateur naturalism is not to be made on the basis of professionalism or even of accuracy. The true naturalist, to put it simply for the moment, is interested in explaining the marvelous; Thoreau's concern is to make the ordinary marvelous.

It is, however, important not to exaggerate, even in methodological terms, the formality of natural history. One of the appeals of the field to Thoreau must have been its realtive flexibility, its potential (and indeed its proven *use*) as a means of gaining personal and even eccentric insight, as a way of proceeding from facts to truth, with neither term of the process being so rigorously limited as to exclude possibilities. In proposing, then, to see what elements of Gilbert White's *Natural History of Selborne* and Darwin's *Voyage of the Beagle* bear particular comparison to Thoreau's works, I am particularly interested in the habits of mind, and the methods of organization of written records or accounts, which allow White and Darwin effectively to write natural history, and what light those habits and methods shed on the peculiar (in several senses) kind of natural history that Thoreau chose to write.

GILBERT WHITE, a country parson, published in 1789 a volume entitled *The Natural History of Selborne*. The book, a collection of letters, the majority on ornithology, might have been expected to be largely ignored; instead, it has become one of the most frequently published books in English. Between 1789 and 1854 (the publication date of the copy Thoreau owned) there were nearly thirty editions, not counting reprintings.[7] White was often used as a standard of comparison for Thoreau, even in his own lifetime, and often with a certain element of regret—Thoreau did not quite seem to measure up. H. S. Canby quotes a letter from Thomas Cholmondeley to Thoreau in 1856, urging him to "Try a history. How if you could write the sweet, beautiful history of Massachusetts? . . . Or take Concord . . . Take the spirit of Walton and a spice of White."[8] Canby describes the letter as "wise"; a later reader might wonder if it did not occur to Thoreau to reply—at least as far as "taking Concord" is concerned—that he had done it. Again, Edward Jones uses the ghost of White as a way of defining the apparent failure of Thoreau's last years: "It was hoped that he would write a natural history of Concord, like White's Natural History of Selborne."[9] What neither comment seems to recognize is how little Thoreau wanted to write a book *like* anyone else's.

The connection between Thoreau and White was made well before 1856. Emerson's preliminary note to his protégé's first important publication, "The Natural History of Massachusetts," uses White and Isaak Walton as part of a jocular and complimentary explanation of how Thoreau came to write the piece: "With all thankfulness we begged our friend to lay down the oar and fishing line, which none can handle better, and assume the pen, that Isaak Walton and White of Selborne might not want a successor, nor the fair meadows, to which we also have owed a home and the happiness of many years, their poet."[10] Hawthorne, whose pages on Thoreau in *The American Notebooks* are such a marvelous short "character" of Thoreau in the early 1840s, seems to have come closest to perceiving the ambiguous relation between the two naturalist writers. Writing to Evert Duyckinck in 1845, in response to the idea that Thoreau might be an author worthy of inclusion in the series of "American Books" which the New York publisher was considering, Hawthorne offered this comment:

> As for Thoreau, there is one chance in a thousand that he might write a most excellent and readable book; but I should be sorry to take the responsibility, either towards you or him, of stirring him up to write anything . . . He is the most unmalleable fellow alive—the narrowest and most notional—and yet, true as all this is, he has great qualities of intellect and character. The only way, however, in which he could ever approach the popular mind, would be by writing a book of simple observation of nature, somewhat in the vein of White's *History of Selborne*.[11]

Hawthorne, seasoned by a longer struggle to be a "popular" or at least a self-supporting writer, had a better grasp of Thoreau's immediate prospects of literary success than did Thoreau himself, or his patron Emerson, at the time. And Hawthorne seems to have understood how far-fetched was the notion that Thoreau could ever, in any simple and direct way, "take the spice of White."

If nothing else, the manner of White's book seems an unlikely model for the most unmalleable fellow alive. There can be few books which combine the astonishing popularity of White's *Selborne* with its extremely deferential and self-effacing manner of presentation. White's first explicit reference to the prospect of turning his letters into an account is typical of the man and the book. He is writing to the second of his correspondents, Daines Barrington:

> When we meet, I shall be glad to have some conversation with you concerning the proposal you make of my drawing up an account of the animals in this neighborhood. Your partiality towards my small abilities persuades you, I fear, that I am able to do more than is in my

power: for it is no small undertaking for a man unsupported and alone to begin a natural history from his own autopsia! Though there is endless room for observation in the field of nature, which is boundless, yet investigation (where a man endeavors to be sure of his facts) can make but slow progress; and all that one could collect in many years would go into a very narrow compass.   (*NHS,* 4/12/1770)[12]

This is partly the diplomacy of literary negotiation, and of friendship-by-letter; and partly too the humility for which Gilbert White is so often praised. But it is more: it is the careful statement of a man with high and serious intentions. The criticism here is directed not only at the small abilities of the particular naturalist, but at the culture of which he is a part, which leaves him alone and unsupported. David Allen summarizes just how accurate is White's observation of the state of natural history in the latter half of the eighteenth century, while at the same time remarking that White's complaint is "a trifle disingenuous," since White's life was not as isolated as we might assume from reading *Selborne.*[13] But it is true that "parochial history" (as White chose to call his effort to "advance natural knowledge" by focusing on one small region; see *NHS,* "Advertisement" and 10/8/1770) is a result of necessity as much as it is of intention. What serves to differentiate White in 1770–1789 from Darwin in 1831–1845 is not only the latter's willingness to undertake a long voyage and his belief that a variety of observation is as valuable as a close look at a small area; the distinction is in large part a question of Darwin's greater *opportunity* to look anywhere but locally.

The passage from *Selborne* raises an important methodological distinction between observation and investigation, and an important formal distinction between observation and an account. On a first reading, we are tempted to describe the book, as a recent editor has, as the "jottings of a rural vicar," fond of looking with a "refreshing ingenuousness" at the local flora and fauna (*NHS,* p. viii). The book presents itself as being without plan, indeed without order in any sense except the accidental one of chronology. It will not do to turn this idea completely on its head, and thereby to claim a tight unity of structure for the work. But *Selborne* is a book with a shape, written by a man with a method, both of which exemplify the approach of the serious amateur and the kind of book he might be expected to produce.

The sequence of letters in the book, on the simplest level, shows a reasonable course of development for a man who became, over the

course of nearly fifteen years, more and more practiced both in observation and in recording that observation. In addition, some three years
after the earliest dated letter in the book, White began to consider the
possibility of publishing; and we should not be surprised if this led
him, in some ways, to think of himself as a writer and not merely a
correspondent. There is, however, a more significant pattern in the
book, significant because closer to a model of "scientific" investigation. We can find at least four reasonably distinct kinds of letters in
Selborne, arranged in a rough sequence leading from data to generalization.

Putting aside for the moment the first nine letters, the book begins
with a kind of letter best represented by Letter **XXXIX** to Thomas
Pennant (*NHS,* 11/9/1773), which covers, in the space of a few pages,
"such observations as may occur," in this case observations of birds.
The character of the letter may be clearly understood from a brief
excerpt:

> The osprey was shot about a year ago at Frinsham-pond, a great lake,
> at about six miles from hence, while it was sitting on the handle of a
> plough and devouring a fish: it used to precipitate itself into the water,
> and so take its prey by surprise.
>
> A great ash-coloured butcher-bird was shot last winter in Tisted-
> park, and a red-backed butcher-bird at Selborne: they are *rarae aves* in
> this country.
>
> Crows go in pairs the whole year round.
>
> Cornish choughs abound, and breed on Beachy-head and on all the
> cliffs of the Sussex coast.

There are clear associative links between the items here. But the letter
can fairly be described as no more than a collection, in the most common sense, of discrete items; White mentions some twenty-four
species in three pages. This stringing together of loosely connected but
precise observations is repeated in a large number of the letters in
Selborne, including most of the letters to Thomas Pennant, and thus
comprises well over a third of the book.

Beginning, however, with the first of the letters to Daines Barrington,[14] the book changes. Letters I and II (*NHS,* 6/30 and 11/2/1769)
consist of an apparently exhaustive list of the birds of Selborne; White
calls the letters an "assemblage of curious and amusing birds" or, a little later, "my little *methodus* of birds." The first description could easily fit the letter to Pennant we have already considered; but the second

phrase carries a clear suggestion of order and regularity that will not suit what has gone on before in the book. The author has moved from collection to catalog, here supported by an apparatus of typography, scientific nomenclature, and systematic categorization.[15] These two letters, the only catalogs in the book, represent a unique but important part of *Selborne,* a form of account that is the substance of much field naturalism, even today.

The third type of letter in *Selborne* is what White calls "monography" (*NHS,* 10/8/1770). These letters, beginning with the sixteenth letter to Barrington (*NHS,* 11/20/1773), are short but coherent essays, usually organized around a single animal. What we have in these letters is still, recognizably, observation, but now formed for the purposes of more complete description and interpretation. The final group of letters consists of essays of a more general sort.[16] It is at this point that the field naturalist, having observed, cataloged, and described one corner of boundless nature, permits himself to reflect either on the goals and methods of his investigation, or on the larger interpretive questions of causality. What White has done, certainly not rigidly and perhaps not intentionally, is to lay out a possible sequence of steps from observation to investigation of the highest sort. *The Natural History of Selborne* can be taken as a kind of guidebook to the method of the field naturalist, who must begin with observation and collection (and must indeed always stay well grounded in these[17]), move to cataloging and categorization, and—only with his facts clearly in hand—proceed to a more developed interpretive description and to generalization about Nature.

This sequence is also a very important model for the proper way to make an account. Despite the apparent randomness which White asserts is the character of his book, even to so "ingenuous" a naturalist as he, simply accumulating and publishing one's notes is not sufficient. Here the introductory letters, the first nine in the book, are important. It is clear that they were added when the remaining letters were being prepared for publication, to provide a general geographical and topographical introduction to Selborne.[18]

The making of a book, then, even so unassuming a book as this one, carries with it a consciousness of form which we must call, however loosely, literary. Darwin, rather more obviously and seriously, exemplifies the same process. His book is usually called a journal, but he himself is careful to point out that it is in fact "a history" written "in

the *form* of a journal" (*Beagle*, xxiii; my italics). It is chiefly this consciousness of what it means to make an account out of what may seem
to the reader often to remain observation of the most direct and unself-
conscious kind, on which in large part I base the assertion that the
literature of natural history may be considered as a distinct genre.
Those who wanted Thoreau to be like Gilbert White seem to have ignored this point. Thoreau might, had he wanted to, have been able to
argue that by trying in his own writings to move from fact to truth he
was indeed following the example, if not precisely the manner, of
Gilbert White. Thoreau's serious intentions as a writer are less removed from the "jottings" of the parson of Selborne than it at first
might appear.

GILBERT WHITE's understanding of the method by which one develops
a proper and useful natural history reveals itself in the rough pattern or
organization and development observable in his book as a whole. The
subject of the naturalist's method is, however, addressed more directly
in the occasional comments White makes in the course of *Selborne*,
especially on the common misdirections into which naturalists have
fallen. Taken as a group, these comments serve to describe a model of
the "parochial historian" and stand as self-defense of the importance of
White's work.

I have already quoted a passage in which White indicates that observation is not an end in itself. But clearly observation is at the heart of
Selborne. Proper observation seems to be the defining characteristic of a
"writer who professes to be an out-door naturalist," one who
therefore "takes his observations from the subject itself, and not from
the writings of others" (*NHS*, 6/30/1769). Later, in discussing what
he feels to be one of his own most surprising observations, he again insists on the necessity of looking carefully at the subject itself: "The fact
that I would advance is, that swifts tread, or copulate, on the wing;
and I would wish any nice observer, that is startled by this supposition, to use his own eyes, and I think he will soon be convinced"
(*NHS*, 9/28/1774). Observation, then, is both the source of information — of facts — and the most reliable test of their accuracy. One of the
commonest failings White sees in other naturalists (and this gentle
cleric is not afraid to play critic) is a willingness to forgo observation.
White calls a common form of this shortcoming "ingenuity": "If one
looks into writers on that subject [species of animals peculiar to

America] little satisfaction is to be found. Ingenious men will readily advance plausible arguments to support whatever theory they shall choose to maintain; but then the misfortune is, every one's hypothesis is each as good as another's, since they are all founded on conjecture" (*NHS,* 5/29/1769). It is not merely a question of ignoring observation in favor of generalization. True observation must be current and personal; "the bane of our science is the comparing one animal to the other by memory," White says (*NHS,* 10/29/1770), arguing, by implication, for careful record-keeping. And the good observer must be active and energetic, in body and mind: "Faunists, as you observe, are too apt to aquiesce in bare descriptions, and a few synonyms: the reason is plain; because all that may be done at home in a man's study, but the investigation of the life and conversation of animals, is a concern of much more trouble and difficulty, and is not to be attained but by the active and inquisitive, and by those that reside much in the country" (*NHS,* 8/1/1771).

White's rejection of "bare descriptions" is an instance of the way, as David Allen puts it, that "the very act of observing natural objects involves a strong aesthetic element which interpenetrates the scientific."[19] And it demonstrates that the question of how to observe cannot be kept separate from the question of how to record and to communicate that observation. What differentiates the "out-door naturalist" from the person who simply enjoys looking at nature is the effort to create a useful written record. Both the naturalist and the pure observer begin, necessarily, with the same task; but the naturalist then needs to assess the validity of his observations and to find a vehicle that will order and record his observations.

We have already seen what White thinks of "memory" — undocumented remembrance. He is no more trusting of what he calls "common report": "There is such a propensity in mankind towards deceiving and being deceived, that one cannot safely relate any thing from common report, especially in print, without expressing some degree of doubt and suspicion"(*NHS,* 11/28/1768). The naturalist, by way of contrast to the generality of mankind, is a part of that group which White repeatedly calls "thinking minds."[20] The avoidance of "deceiving and being deceived" is fundamental to the kind of thinking White values. Answering one of Pennant's questions concerning bird migration, he writes: "Was not candour and openness the very life of natural history, I should pass over this query just as the sly commentator does over a crabbed passage in a classic; but common ingenuousness obliges me to confess, not without some degree of shame, that I only reasoned in that case from analogy" (*NHS*, 8/30/1769). The modern reader might wonder just what is White ashamed of, since neither reasoning nor analogy seem to be especially baneful traits. But throughout the book White is especially distrustful of analogy. Several months later he raises the point again: "Though I delight very little in analogous reasoning, knowing how fallacious it is with respect to natural history; yet, in the following instance, I cannot help being inclined to think it may conduce towards the explanation of a difficulty I have mentioned before" (*NHS*, 12/8/1769). It will not do to exaggerate White's attitude toward analogy. His distrust does not keep him from employing it, both here and later.[21] What he disapproves of is not the use of analogy as a way of moving from fact to interpretation, but analogous reasoning as a habit of mind which always and too easily prefers generalization and which reasons too often in the absence of fact.

Again and again, White insists on the centrality of the facts, and on the primacy of the task of collecting facts carefully and at first hand. This forms the basis of his definition of parochial history and monography: "Monographers, come from whence they may, have, I think, fair pretence to challenge some regard and approbation from the lovers of natural history; for, as no man can alone investigate all the works of nature, these partial writers may, each in their department, be more accurate in their discoveries, and freer from errors, than more general writers; and so by degrees may pave the way to an universal correct natural history" (*NHS*, 9/14/1770). Or, as he puts it in one of the early letters to Barrington: "Men that undertake only one district are much more likely to advance general knowledge than those that grasp at more than they can possibly be acquainted with: every kingdom, every province, should have its own monographer" (*NHS*, 10/8/1770). It is an argument which Thoreau, reading White during the final stages of putting together his own undertakings in one small district of Massachusetts, must have found familiar and reassuring.

And an important part of that reassurance—since Thoreau had the ambition to be, not just a modest paver of the way, but an original force—must have been that parochial history, even if well begun by White, had not yet been done on the right premises. White, as suits a self-effacing clergyman, acknowledges the inevitable limitations of human knowledge and the boundlessness of God's creation, nature.

The great puzzles are, as White puts it, both a delight and a mortification (*NHS*, 2/28/1769): a delight because they show the hand of
the Creator; a mortification because they remind the observer of his
own distance from that Creator. That is too orthodox a position to
suit Thoreau: on the one hand, because he is never quite satisfied until
he has found and measured the bottom; on the other hand, because he
wants his puzzles to produce unsettling, not acceptable, lessons.

To be fair to White, he is no less interested than Thoreau in pursu-
ing mysteries until they yield answers. His delight and mortification
when forced to admit how little he knows about bird migration in
1769 does not, of course, keep him from continuing to investigate the
problem (*NHS*, 2/12/1771). White's belief that the collection of local
facts is important rests on the idea that it is only a first step; there is
something (call it "knowledge" or "universal correct natural history,"
or, to use Thoreau's word, "truth") beyond the facts, which must
always be kept in sight, if only as a distant goal.

In other words, an overemphasis on White the observer tends to
obscure the degree to which he proposes generalized explanations.
Facts are to him most useful when they can be accumulated and
employed — often by means of the application of that troublesome
tool, analogy — to propound hypotheses about the workings of nature.
And he has a clear if not altogether explicit idea of how this movement
from fact to truth can be accomplished. He devotes, for example, his
Letter XXXVI to Barrington (*NHS*, 11/22/1777) to a consideration
of the effect of temperature on the reawakening of nature in spring.
First he assembles his observations, both from a useful recent circum-
stance (an unexpected and early warm spell during the preceding
March) and from years spent watching the life of Selborne, as recorded
in "my journals for many years past." In the end, he can move to a
generalization about hibernation:

> From all these circumstances laid together, it is obvious that torpid in-
> sects, reptiles, and quadrupeds, are awakened from their profoundest
> slumbers by a little untimely warmth; and therefore that nothing so
> much promotes this death-like stupor as a defect of heat. And farther, it
> is reasonable to suppose that two whole species, or at least many in-
> dividuals of those two species, of British *hirundines* [swallows] do never
> leave this island at all, but partake of the same benumbed state . . .

White has his Shandean side; his hobby-horse is swallows and their
migratory habits. But clearly, whatever the subject, this is analogous

reasoning rightly done. It is what, in White's view, permits the thinking mind at least to begin making a natural history "from his own autopsia"; it is his exemplification of how facts blossom into truth.

The process, in its elaborated written form, can be broken down into four steps. White's Letter XXXVII to Barrington is the most clear-cut example (*NHS*, 1/8/1778). The letter begins with a striking observation: "There was in this village several years ago a miserable pauper, who, from his birth, was afflicted with a leprosy, as far as we are aware of a singular kind, since it affected only the palms of his hands and the soles of his feet." It would appear that the letter might go on to explain this "singular kind" of affliction. White, who as we have seen has a low opinion of what is now called folk wisdom, gives an example of "common report": "The good women, who love to account for every defect in children by the doctrine of longing, said that his mother felt a violent propensity for oysters, which she was unable to gratify." White does not take the time to demolish this "account," perhaps because it is so outlandish on its face.[22] And in any case, it is off the main track. We might observe however that what is particularly wrong about the way the good women approach the problem is simplistic analogizing; the explanation which White will go on to suggest is not a matter of a single and universal cause, but of a complex of causative factors.

White proceeds, by a graceful association of ideas, to move closer to his real question. He undertakes a brief survey of the evidence for the premise that "leprosy has made dreadful havoc among mankind." He is still, I think, collecting, although now he uses, not first-hand observation, but written records: the Bible first, an unchallengeable source; then the less specific record of the "large provision" made by "our forefathers . . . for objects laboring under this calamity" of leprosy. The reliance on the evidence of history is, in *Selborne* as it is customarily printed, somewhat anomalous; but, as we will see shortly, it is not at all alien to White's purpose in writing "parochial history."

Finally he reaches the main point: "It must therefore, in these days, be, to an humane and thinking person, a matter of equal wonder and satisfaction, when he contemplates how nearly this pest is eradicated, and observes that a leper now is a rare sight." As I have tried to indicate, the statement is characteristic, both in its reference to the thinking person, and in the balance of wonder and satisfaction — a brighter instance of the delight and mortification he mentions elsewhere. What he has done is to move from observation to generalization, and generalization of a particular kind. There is a puzzle to be solved: "He [the humane and thinking person] will, moreover, when engaged in such a train of thought, naturally inquire for the reason." Immediately White offers four possibilities: "This happy change perhaps may have originated and been continued from the much smaller quantity of salted meat and fish now eaten in these kingdoms; from the use of linen next the skin; from the plenty of better bread; and from the profusion of roots, legumes, and greens, so common in every family." We can see now that the good women were not quite so far from the truth as it might at first seem; diet is closely involved with the solution White propounds. Having made his proposal, White looks for corroboration. He casts a broad net, accumulating evidence from old books ("the marvelous account . . . of the eldest Spencer in the days of Edward the Second"), from common personal experience (the "memory" of "every middle-aged person of observation"), and from the records of other observers, especially his favorite among the fathers of natural history, John Ray.

The sequence of steps, from observation to generalization to explanation to corroboration, is an essential and familiar one; it is the usual method in those sciences which rely more on observation than on experimentation. And the range of reference is equally essential. The book which the modern reader is most likely to encounter as *The Natural History of Selborne* is in fact only a part of what White set before the public in 1789. His full title was *The Natural History and Antiquities of Selborne in the County of Southampton.* Most of his editors have omitted the antiquities, often with a dismissal such as Richard Mabey's: "I have not included the *Antiquities* . . . They have little in common with the *Natural History* either in quality or originality, and do little more than blunt the extraordinary pitch of condensation which White has achieved in his one true book" (*NHS,* p. xxvii).[23] In other words, like Thoreau, White seems to have attracted editors who are convinced they have a clearer image of the book the author intended to write than did the author himself. The suppression of the *Antiquities* ignores the degree to which White intended the apparently separate fields of naturalism and antiquarianism to stand together. He made the connection explicit in an "Advertisement" which he prepared as a preface to the first edition of *Selborne:* "The Author of the following letters takes the liberty, with all proper deference, of laying before the public his idea of *parochial history,* which, he thinks, ought to consist of natural productions and occurences as well as antiquities. He is also of the opinion that if stationary men would pay some attention to the districts in which they reside, and would publish their thoughts respecting the objects that surround them, from such materials might be drawn the most complete county-histories" (*NHS*, p. 3).

It is this broad notion of natural history, a paying of attention to the past *and* the present, firmly based in the local and the immediate but not refusing any possible source until it has been assessed and weighed, which can stand as a home, in literary terms, for *Walden* and for much else of Thoreau's work. It would indeed have been fitting if Thoreau had read this preface when, nearing the end of his reshaping of the experience of life at Walden into a suitable account, he read (or reread) *Selborne*; it appears, however, that he did not have before him White's explicit argument for the synthesis of history and natural history.[24] But the same synthesis is present even in those portions of *Selborne* which are normally called simply "natural history." And it is a synthesis which rests well alongside the peculiarly mixed books of natural history produced or planned by the mature Thoreau.

WHATEVER the similarities of method between Gilbert White and Thoreau—similarities which I will try to detail further in later chapters—there is an important distinction in intention between the two writers. Both men set for themselves the task of moving from facts to truth; but the kind of truth most commonly sought after in *Selborne* is not the kind to be found in *Walden*. White's progress, when he leaves pure observation, is always toward explanation. In his Letter XXIII to Barrington (*NHS*, 6/8/1775), White recalls, for instance, a truly marvelous experience: "About nine an appearance very unusual began to demand our attention, a shower of cobwebs falling from very elevated regions, and continuing, without any interruption, till the close of the day. These webs were not single filmy threads, floating in the air in all directions, but perfect flakes or rags; some near an inch broad, and five or six long, which fall with a degree of velocity which showed they were considerably heavier than the atmosphere." The careful measurement and description, and the calm and discreet presentation, cannot disguise the peculiarity of what is being observed. Like the curious leper of Selborne, this is a puzzle.

Confronted with the marvelous, White's first impulse is always to reject superstition and to insist on the possibility of a reasonable explanation. So, in this case, he remarks: "Strange and superstitious as the notions about [the cobwebs] were formerly, nobody in these days doubts but that they are the real production of small spiders, which swarm in the fields in fine weather in autumn, and have a power of shooting out webs from their tails so as to render themselves buoyant, and lighter than air." He is careful, we notice, to define precisely what the mystery is—not the source of the webs, but how they come to make up an anomalous fall. And he is not afraid to admit the limitations of his own thought; exactly how these spiders produce the cobwebs is, he admits, a "matter beyond my skill." He goes on, however, to "hazard a supposition": that the webs, expelled by the spiders, are drawn up into the air "by a brisk evaporation" of the dew. Lest we think that this is a wild guess, White again seeks corroboration—in this case, from a former Royal Physician and from his own quotidian experience while "reading in the parlor." White is, of course, prepared to stand in wonder before the mysteries of Providence and Nature; but he assumes that, in the end, there is an explanation to be found, and found in the most mundane of circumstances, when they are subjected to careful observation and thought.

This assumption that the marvelous can be explained is clearly a part of Thoreau's mental hardware. He is unforgiving, after all, toward those who do not take the trouble to measure "bottomless" ponds (*Walden*, 177–178). But Thoreau combines with this approach its opposite; one of his favorite turns of mind is to find in the ordinary something susceptible of being made into myth. On the beach at Cape Cod, for instance, he mixes the observations of the field naturalist with something quite different. His description of the Clay Ponds in North Truro (*Cape Cod*, 164–170) could, without much alteration of style or manner, be included in *Selborne* or Darwin's *Voyage;* it is full of number, detail, and careful scientific naming. And he puts aside common superstition, often quite tersely, as in his treatment of the folk tales of the "tenth wave" (pp. 157–158). But he will not undermine the fabulous tale told by a lighthouse keeper, of a day when the sun stood still (pp. 173–174).

Earlier, on another beach, Thoreau goes salvaging (p. 117). He lists what he and his companion found—a "box or barrel," a "valuable cord and buoy, part of a seine." Finally he remarks, apparently off-handedly, "I picked up a bottle half buried in the wet sand." He continues his description in a straightforward way, although there has been enough talk before this in his excursion about wrecks and their significance to make us suspect he has more than bottles on his mind. The bottle is "covered with barnacles, but stoppled tight, and half full of red ale, which still smacked of juniper." Now, however, the observer begins to give way to the grinder of metaphors. The bottle is "all that remained I fancied from the wreck of a rowdy world—that great salt sea on the one hand, and this little sea of ale on the other, preserving their separate characters." We are tempted here—as we never are in reading Gilbert White—to suspect word-play. The observation has moved to "fancy"; and at the same time, the speaker's desired distance from the rowdy world is suggested by the implication that all he fancies of that world is a half-empty bottle.

The possibility of using this bottle as the basis of a careful and reasoned investigation of the sort White builds on the tale of a leper or a rain of cobwebs is still not altogether gone; we might be about to turn to the question of the persistence of some odors, or the peculiar action of ocean currents, or the resistance of glass to saltwater. But of course Thoreau has an altogether different purpose in mind: "What if it could tell us its adventures over countless ocean waves! Man would not be man through such ordeals as it had passed. But as I poured it slowly out on to the sand, it seemed to me that man himself was like a half-emptied bottle of pale ale, which Time had drunk so far, yet stoppled tight for a while, and drifting about in the ocean of circumstances, but destined ere-long to mingle with the surrounding waves, or be spilled amid the sands of a distant shore." The truth which here blossoms from an unprepossessing fact is not scientific explanation; it is a part of an elaborated metaphor of sea and land, time and man, which runs throughout Thoreau's excursion on the Cape. And it is anchored in a piece of partly jocular self-mythography; Thoreau has, quietly, made a Titan of himself. What even the countless ocean waves cannot do, what indeed only personified Time can do, and that slowly, Thoreau himself manages almost without our noticing it; for it is he who mixes the "separate characters" of the two seas, small and large, by pouring the ale on to the sand.

If then we are going to call Thoreau a natural historian, we will have to qualify the description, or add to it the equally important title of parabolist. When he comes, in *Walden, Cape Cod,* and elsewhere, to render his accounts, he will not do it so ingenuously as did Gilbert White. But the naturalist need not, after all, be quite so ingenuous as the vicar of Selborne; for evidence of this, we need to look at the naturalist of the *Beagle.*

IN JUNE OF 1851, Thoreau read Darwin's *Voyage of the Beagle* with considerable attention. His notes on the book, consisting primarily of excerpts and paraphrases, occupy some fourteen pages of his published journal.[25] A few of the excerpts were reused by Thoreau later, in *Walden* (p. 12) and in *Cape Cod* (pp. 40, 122, 127). The case, then, for considering Thoreau and Darwin together is stronger than was the case for the pairing of Thoreau and Gilbert White, to whom Thoreau, as far as I can tell, does not refer at all in his published writings, and to whom the references in the journal are brief, few, and scattered.[26]

But still there is not enough evidence to argue in favor of a direct line of influence. What is significant, and of course understandable on purely chronological grounds, is that Thoreau's contact with Darwin is at this point solely through the *Voyage;* only, that is, with "Darwin the naturalist" (*Walden,* 12). David Allen describes Darwin's unique combination of "two contrasting types that are normally quite separate: as well as collector and observer he was an experimenter and theorist."[27] By the time *Origin of Species* appeared and had its effect, Darwin was as professional a scientist as the age could offer.[28] But the Darwin of the *Beagle* was nothing of the sort. The young ex-medical student and prospective (but not enthusiastically so) minister who signed on in some scientific capacity for the surveying voyage of H.M.S. *Beagle* in 1831 was a gifted amateur, whose preparation for a life of science was, to say the least, erratic.[29] Darwin himself, in introducing the reader to the revised (and most widely read) edition of the *Voyage* (1845), was careful to distinguish between his "sketch" and "the larger publications, which comprise the scientific results of the Expedition" — larger publications which he then lists, and which prove to be, in most cases, by other "distinguished authors" including Darwin's mentor and sponsor, Henslow (*Beagle* xxiii–xxiv).

The criterion of professionalism, then, need not have kept Thoreau from finding in Darwin's book not only raw material, but a literary parallel to his own work. And indeed it is a surprise, to one whose only experience with Darwin's prose is the often fearsome and ponderous complexity of *Origin of Species,* to find how enjoyable the *Voyage* is. It is writing of a kind which, as has been shown by John Aldrich Christie, Thoreau found especially appealing, a combination of field naturalism, personal narrative, travelogue, speculation, and history. Here, even more obviously than in the case of Gilbert White, the inclusiveness of natural history writing is apparent, an inclusiveness that considers mountain vistas, the Brazilian slave system, condors, Argentinian politics, Indian names, South Sea missionaries, coral reefs, Noah's flood, the state of the English nation, Handel's music, the future of manufactures in Australia, Humboldt's *Voyages,* and, of course, the vast problem of the development and disappearance of animal species, all to be readily available for description, comment, and reference.

But Darwin's journal also shows at least some of the ways in which this inclusive, not to say motley and undefined, range of subject matter can be *formed.* That Darwin's book is a much more evidently organized book than Gilbert White's is, of course, in large part a result of its having the advantage of geography and chronology as shaping devices. "Parochial history" cannot so easily avail itself of the tools of travelogue. *Walden* may be unique among parochial histories in managing to do so, to be a squatter's travelogue, a voyage of discovery, not to the Galapagos and Tahiti, but within an area even smaller than Selborne. But we should not allow ourselves to be so bedazzled by the geographic range of the *Voyage* as to ignore the fact that Darwin and White, when attempting to write natural history, engage in recognizably the same kinds of writing.

Like *Selborne,* Darwin's *Voyage* can be analyzed into its constituent elements of raw observation, catalog, monography, and speculative essay. These elements are not, however, arranged even in the rough progression which I have tried to describe in *Selborne.* Darwin's history in the form of a journal moves readily within chapters from one kind of writing to another. The summary offered by Darwin for Chapter XVII, recording his visit to the Galapagos, shows the variety that is usual in the book:

> Galapagos Archipelago—The whole Group Volcanic—Number of Craters—Leafless Bushes—Colony at Charles Island—James Island—Salt-lake in Crater—Natural History of the Group—Ornithology, curious Finches—Reptiles—Great Tortoises, habits of—Marine Lizard, feeds on Sea-weed—Terrestrial Lizard, burrowing habits, herbivorous—Importance of Reptiles in the Archipelago—Fish, Shells, Insects—Botany—American type of organization—Differences in the Species or Races on different Islands—Tameness of the Birds—Fear of Man, an acquired instinct. (*Beagle,* xxx)

This is the substance of fewer than thirty pages out of some three hundred; it might appear that the sheer accumulation of detail would produce the kind of loose association of facts we found in Gilbert White's

Letter XXXIX. But the chapter is clearly organized. It opens with two detailed paragraphs of general description of the islands — number, size, location, geologic character and formation, and climate (*Beagle,* 373–374). Then it proceeds to first-hand observation, beginning on "the morning (17th [of September, 1835]) we landed on Chatham Island" (p. 374) and following, in chronological order, Darwin's explorations of Chatham, Charles, and James islands (pp. 374–378). It is only after presenting what we might call his fieldwork that Darwin turns specifically to the "natural history of these islands" (p. 378), a turn of phrase that suggests that he, even more than Gilbert White, would insist that natural history is not only or even primarily pure observation.

Now Darwin turns cataloger, although always with an eye toward supplemental comment, especially on the subject which proves to be the crucial issue of the chapter and indeed of the whole voyage: the development and distribution of species. But, as he reminds his readers, "no one has a right to speculate without distinct facts" (*Beagle,* 379), and the progress of the chapter exemplifies how to ground speculation properly. It is only after his listing of the fauna and (more briefly) flora of the islands that he turns to "the most remarkable feature in the natural history of this archipelago": the surprising fact that each island seems to contain distinct species (p. 394). It would be inaccurate to suggest that Darwin immediately begins to speculate; the full fruit of his observation took over twenty years to develop, a long wait indeed for the facts to blossom. What he does is much closer to what he later said he understood to be "that [in which] science consists": "grouping facts so that general laws or conclusions may be drawn from them."[30] In the late 1830s and 1840s, while he was writing and revising the *Voyage,* all he could manage were some provisional groupings; the general laws are not yet apparent. His conclusion is to dismiss as inadequate the readily available explanations, based on soil, topography, climate, or "the general character of the associated beings" (p. 398). The chapter ends, not with a resolution of the puzzle, but with a turn to a different subject entirely— a short monograph on the tameness of birds (pp. 398–401).[31]

Perhaps the only occasion in the book when Darwin allows himself (or when he feels his data will allow him) to undertake a broad explanatory essay is when, in Chapter XIX, he inserts a lengthy discussion of coral reefs— an account which, as he acknowledges in a footnote, was prepared and read separately as a series of two papers for the Geological Society (p. 464). In other words, the young Darwin, Thoreau's "Darwin the naturalist," like Gilbert White, spends much of his time paving the way for "universal correct natural history." The *Voyage,* like *Selborne,* contains a preponderance of observation and catalog and, relatively speaking, a dearth of speculation.

Still, the assumption is clear—that there *is* explanation to be found, if only in the long run; and that the correct habitual movement of intellect is from perception (often accompanied by wonder and puzzlement) to clear, detailed, reasonable description, and thence to explanation. The difference between White and Darwin rests, in part, on the intervention of that general shift of mind we call Romanticism. It shows itself, as nowhere else, in the way Darwin repeatedly seeks out the grand and sublime, most frequently (and we might say, symptomatically) from the top of a mountain:

> I continued slowly to advance for an hour along the broken and rocky banks, and was amply repaid by the grandeur of the scene. The gloomy depth of the ravine well accorded with the universal signs of violence. On every side were lying irregular masses of rocky and torn-up trees; other trees, though still erect, were decayed to the heart and ready to fall. The entangled mass of the thriving and the fallen reminded me of the forests within the tropics—yet there was a difference: for in these still solitudes, Death instead of Life, seemed the predominant spirit. I followed the watercourse till I came to a spot, where a great slip had cleared a straight space down the mountain side. By this road I ascended to a considerable elevation, and obtained a good view of the surrounding woods. (*Beagle,* 210)

On another occasion, Darwin makes his debt to Romanticism explicit by concluding a description of a scene of "stillness and desolation" with three lines of verse:

> None can reply—all seems eternal now.
> The wilderness has a mysterious tongue,
> Which teaches awful doubt.

He helpfully provides a footnote to identify the lines as Shelley's (p. 169).[32]

That our naturalist sees the ravines of Tierra del Fuego very much as Shelley saw the Vale of Chaumonix should, at the very least, disabuse us of our belief in the stereotype of the clinical, objective, "scientific" observer; good naturalism need not displace passion or awe. Indeed, it is the direction in which he *proceeds* from awe that identifies the naturalist, even in his elevated moments. Darwin's description of the Fuegian ravine, for example, continues:

> By this road I ascended to a considerable elevation, and obtained a good view of the surrounding woods. The trees all belong to one kind, the Fagus betulloides; for the number of other species of Fagus and of the Winter's Bark, is quite inconsiderable. This beech keeps its leaves throughout the year; but its foliage is of a peculiar brownish-green colour, with a tinge of yellow. As the whole landscape is thus coloured, it has a sombre, dull appearance; nor is it often enlivened by the rays of the sun. (*Beagle*, 210)

The "degree of mysterious grandeur" (p. 211) which the naturalist finds in the scene can be, if not precisely explained, then at least analyzed in a recognizably scientific way. In his final chapter, "Retrospect," Darwin explains that detailed observation is not the enemy, but the source of enjoyment: "I am strongly induced to believe that, as in music, the person who understands every note will, if he also possesses a proper taste, more thoroughly enjoy the whole, so he who examines each part of a fine view, may also thoroughly comprehend the full and combined effect" (p. 500). It is important to realize that the repeated movement in the *Voyage* from wonder to detail does not necessarily imply an absolute preference for the latter; any more than Thoreau's interest in literally measuring the bottom of Walden Pond deprives him of the opportunity later of suggesting the virtues of bottomlessness (*Walden*, 287).

Still, the observation of beech trees, the examination of each part, its name, its color, its natural history, does in Darwin's book serve to tame the sublime; and in this we can set Thoreau apart from Darwin, White, and other more traditional naturalists. Here is Darwin, just ashore on the Galapagos, facing and describing the "Cyclopean scene," the most striking element of which is a great number of "black truncated cones":

> From one small eminence I counted sixty of them, all surmounted by craters more or less perfect. The greater number consisted merely of a ring of red scoriae or slags, cemented together, and their height above the plain of lava was not more than from fifty to a hundred feet: none had been very lately active. . . . From the regular form of the many

craters, they gave to the country an artificial appearance, which vividly reminded me of those parts of Staffordshire, where the great iron-foundries are most numerous . . . As I was walking along I met two large tortoises, each of which must have weighed at least two hundred pounds: one was eating a piece of cactus, and as I approached, it stared at me and slowly stalked away; the other gave a deep hiss, and drew in its head. These huge reptiles . . . seemed to my fancy like some antediluvian animals.   (*Beagle*, 375–376)

Explicitly, the description could not be clearer, nor the fact of the strangeness of the scene more openly admitted. Implicitly, it is a set-piece of the methods of familiarizing the marvelous. The use of number, and especially of detailed measurement is one device; the reliance on precise technical language ("scoriae or slags") is another. The comparisons employed move from the distant and unfamiliar to the nearby and familiar; the iron foundries might be, to other eyes, Satanic mills, but they are at the very least recognizable and manmade. The nearly comic indifference of the beasts, so unthreatening as to prefer cactus to humanity, so timid as to withdraw before an unarmed man, is a sample of the kind of reassuring observation at which Darwin is especially adept; the mundane introduction of these antediluvian beasts ("As I was walking along I met . . . ") moves them a little closer to the Strand than to Chaos. And the imaginative possibilities of the antediluvian atmosphere are quietly undercut even as they are introduced, by the use of simile rather than metaphor and by the choice of "fancy," with its connotations of passing whim. Again and again in the *Voyage* Darwin manages the same trick of analyzing and familiarizing the exotic and the mysterious.[33]

And he does so, not only by means of his habitual progress of mind from the sublime to the particular and by his use of a style built on number, name, measure, and explanation, but also by his very presence on the scene. Both the *Voyage* and *Selborne* are, to some degree, personal narratives. But White, while relying on personal observation, is at the same time curiously impersonal. It would be hard, from interval evidence, to describe the "I" of *Selborne*, beyond a few generalities about geniality and charm. The narrator of the *Voyage* is, on the other hand, a definite and recognizable character; and a man likely to enlist our sympathies and belief, assuming we are capable of putting ourselves back in time and space to the England of the young Victoria. It is not too many pages into the book before we realize we are in the company of a bright and observant young man, a canny tourist with an eye for saving a penny; knowledgeable in the arts, a moralist (both about nature and about human issues such as slavery), sportsman, patriot; diplomatic and courteous, possessed of sound, progressive (but never radical) views on politics and religion;[34] a man of taste and some fastidiousness, but adventurous, curious, and able to make a joke at his own expense; a man who, in spite of a genteel upbringing, has a good sense of business and the management of men. Of course, Darwin does not, overtly and in one place, so describe himself. To assemble the clues whereby the portrait may be derived would be possible (and most of the evidence could be found in the first third of the book), but it would be a cumbersome task. He does not wish to call attention to himself; nor do I mean to suggest that this is a fabricated creature, a persona developed for polemical or purely literary purposes. It is apparently the way Darwin was.[35] But the presence, as our guide and explicator, of such a reassuring person in the midst of the wildest scenes and of literally earth-shaking natural phenomena, is a major reason why, in reading the book, we can face even the solitude in which "Death instead of Life, seemed the predominant spirit" without our wonder becoming terror.

And here there is an important irony in the analogies I have been trying to outline between the methods of natural history and the writing of Thoreau. It is clear that, to whatever degree he shares the interests of the true naturalist, Thoreau wants to take an original stand. In many ways his purposes are almost exactly opposite to those of White or Darwin. He wants to unsettle (to brag loud enough to wake his neighbors), not to reassure; to confuse, not to analyze and explain. His central moments on Walden Pond are those times when he can no longer distinguish up from down, air from water. He knows that an essential element in the way we read and understand personal narrative is the character of the narrator; it is arguable that this element is often more important than *what* the narrator says. He need not—indeed, he certainly did not—learn this from Darwin's *Voyage of the Beagle*. But one can imagine his pleasure, in reading a work centered on so pleasant and affable a person, in being convinced again that the same device could be put to opposite ends. His first note on Darwin (*Journal*, II, 228) uses Darwin's observation of guinea fowl to make a personal, anecdotal metaphor, the brunt of which is, "keep your distance."[36] The same feisty, individualistic mood informs

Walden. So it appears that a personal narrative of natural history which intends to wake the neighbors might indeed function in large measure because the "I" of the book is almost Darwin's polar opposite—by the world's standards, unsound, uncommon, even unsympathetic, one of those "strong and valiant natures, who will mind their own affairs whether in heaven or hell" and who therefore stand utterly removed from "the mass of men . . . most terribly impoverished" (*Walden,* 16).

If there is anything to be gained by calling Thoreau a natural historian, it must be qualified by the observation that, unlike Darwin or White, whose primary interest is in fact, Thoreau longs for (and strives to make) parables; and parables of the dark sort suggested by Mark IV:10–12: "And when he was alone, those who were about him with the twelve asked him concerning the parables. And he said to them, 'To you has been given the secret of the kingdom of God, but for those outside everything is in parables; so that they may indeed see but not perceive, and may indeed hear but not understand; lest they should turn again, and be forgiven.'" Thoreau's version of this is to be found in the concluding chapter of *Walden:*

> It is a ridiculous demand which England and America make, that you shall speak so that they can understand you. Neither men nor toad-stools grow so. As if it were important and there were not enough to understand you without them . . . I desire to speak somewhere *without* bounds; like a man in a waking moment, to men in their waking moments . . . I do not suppose that I have attained to obscurity, but I should be proud if no more fatal fault were found with my pages on this score than was found with the Walden ice.   (*Walden,* 324–325)

A writer who would speak without bounds is not likely to accept readily any of the more apparent critical labels; and Thoreau certainly does not. A writer who hopes to attain obscurity is a writer working in a direction opposite to that of Gilbert White and Charles Darwin. But the divergence of intention does not necessarily imply an equal divergence in *method.*

Indeed, it is more than possible that the methods of the natural historian were so profound and automatic a part of Thoreau's thinking that they affected not only the material and shape of his writing but the very way in which he composed those writings. If we recall

Darwin's definition of science—"grouping facts so that general laws or conclusions may be drawn from them"—and Gilbert White's equivalent use of the image of "laying circumstances together" to reach an hypothesis, there is a striking parallel to Thoreau's description of his method of making a book. In 1856 Thoreau's friend, Harrison Blake, asked Thoreau to lecture in Worcester. Thoreau's refusal sets out both his customary method of composition, and its besetting flaw:

> I have not for a long time been putting such thoughts together as I should like to read to the company you speak of. I have enough of that sort to say, or even read, but not time now to arrange it . . . In fine, what I have is either too scattered or loosely arranged, or too light, or else too scientific and matter of fact (I run a good deal into that of late) for so hungry a company.
>
> I am still a learner, not a teacher, feeding somewhat omnivorously, browsing both stalk & leaves; but I shall perhaps be enabled to speak with the more precision & authority by & by,—if philosophy and sentiment are not buried under a multitude of details. (*Correspondence*, 423–424; 21 May 1856)

The fear of burial under facts is a familiar one. The means of escape, we notice, is not the avoidance of detail but a proper arrangement. "Putting such thoughts together" is in this case not merely a politely self-effacing locution; it is a reasonable short description of the way in which Thoreau mined his journal for the material of his developed works. Perry Miller and J. L. Shanley have each, for very different reasons, attempted to describe Thoreau's method of writing.[37] Shanley, in particular, documents Thoreau's use of scattered elements of his journal in the construction of the first version of *Walden*. Miller, from a much more antagonistic viewpoint, offers this description of Thoreau at work:

> Margaret Fuller, to express her dislike of it, called [it] a "mosaic." Thoreau builds his edifice out of bricks already baked. Contemporaries objected that the *Week* was a pastiche of bits previously printed, mostly in *The Dial*, stuck together by the artificial glue of the voyage. Some who noticed *Walden* sensed that it also was a conglomeration; such, in great part, it is. But in this one instance, and only this one, the devouring forces of ego and anxiety struck a balance; the pellets consolidated in expectation of a whole proved to be more than parts of a part.[38]

The passage is hardly Miller at his best. Entrapped in his own metaphor (who, after all, builds with unbaked bricks?) and nearly desperate to find a suitably dismissive word for the material in the journal (bricks, bits, pellets), he nevertheless points out Thoreau's method of culling the record of his observations and then laying what had been separate passages alongside one another—a process parallel to the methodological prescriptions of White and Darwin.

It is, as Miller observes and as Thoreau was terribly aware, a method full of risk, especially for a man of letters. It cannot be denied that there are, in Thoreau's works, frequent cases in which the glue is not only artificial and visible, but also, in the end, ineffectual. Worse yet—and it is this that is the basis of the common but inaccurate estimation of Thoreau's last years as years of failure—there is the danger that one might become so buried in detail that no productive collocation is possible or attempted. To a natural historian this burial is, if sad, still not utterly damning. Gilbert White knows that he has done little more in *Selborne* than gather information. But since such gathering is a necessary first step toward the more elaborated and profound understanding which he considers to be the end of natural history, White can be satisfied to be a simple husbandman. The proper use of the method of collection is of sufficient importance to him that the ultimate goal, a universal correct natural history, can be left to others.

Thoreau's comments on the usefulness of collections such as the one he reviews in "The Natural History of Massachusetts" acknowledge the possibility that the observer may not himself be able to proceed to a larger understanding. Thoreau's reading of naturalists, antiquaries, and travelers, from whose accumulation of detail he himself derived the pieces of larger interpretations, seemed to bear this out. He observes, in summarizing his qualified approval of "volumes" which "deal much in measurements and minute descriptions," that "the ground was comparatively unbroken, and we will not complain of the pioneer, if he raises no flowers with his first crop" (*Excursions,* 130). But he himself is not willing, as Gilbert White is, to be only such a breaker of ground; he wants his crop too, and not only beans. Considering in his journal (V, 4–5, March 5, 1853), whether he can justly apply to himself the title of scientist, even "using the term science in the most comprehensive sense possible," Thoreau insists that he is interested in a "science which deals with the higher law." Finding no such science about him, Thoreau (he is in one of his saintly, not to say arrogant, moods) tries "to speak to their [common scientists'] condition and describe to them that poor part of me which alone they can understand." The names which Thoreau can find for himself, in the language of fallen man, are "mystic, transcendentalist, and natural philosopher to boot."

He distinguishes himself from the common run of scientist/naturalists, then, by the loftiness of his aspirations. But he does not thereby reject the task or method of the naturalist, although he cannot happily rest in the role of observer and collector. Even when facts no longer seem to bloom for him, he does not altogether lose faith in his method of "association" or "juxtaposition." His fullest account of how the method should work is to be found in a journal entry of 1852:

> To set down such choice experiences that my own writings may inspire me and at last I may make wholes of parts. Certainly it is a distinct profession to rescue from oblivion and to fix the sentiments and thoughts which visit all men more or less generally, that the contemplation of the unfinished picture may suggest its harmonious completion. Associate reverently and as much as you can with your loftiest thoughts. Each thought that is welcomed and recorded is a nest egg, by the side of which more will be laid. Thoughts accidentally thrown together become a frame in which more may be developed and exhibited. Perhaps this is the main value of a habit of writing, of keeping a journal,—that so we remember our best hours and stimulate ourselves . . . Having by chance recorded a few disconnected thoughts and then brought them into juxtaposition, they suggest a whole new field in which it was possible to labor and to think. Thought begat thought. (*Journal*, III, 217; Jan. 22, 1852)

It is the method of the naturalist applied to the mind and the self: observe, record, arrange, understand. And it is a method which Thoreau connects verbally with an almost religious sense of vocation—"associate reverently . . . here is profession enough."

Thoreau, then, will not, with good reason, accept unequivocally the name of natural historian; but at the same time he will not deny himself the use of the methods of that "profession." In the same journal entry in which he calls himself mystic and transcendentalist, he concludes by insisting that it is "absurd that, though I probably stand as near to nature as any of them [the world's scientists], and am by constitution as good an observer as most, yet a true account of my relation to nature should excite their ridicule only!" (*Journal*, V, 5). As always, he asserts his claims as observer and student, but only on his own individualistic terms.

It remains to be investigated precisely what sort of accounts a naturalist who writes dark parable will render. That investigation will take us eventually to *Walden* and to *Cape Cod,* a parochial history and a travelogue, a book by a squatter and one by a stranger, a book about saintliness and one about purgatory, and in the latter case a book which includes Thoreau's most direct extended effort to evaluate the methods and materials of a more customary sort of historiography. We will find in both of these books, and not always at the most expected moments, the methods of the natural historian. And we can place these works, and indeed most of Thoreau's writing, within a distinct (and in Thoreau's day, flourishing) genre of writing which also bears the name natural history.

· 3 ·

NOMEN
GENERALISSIMUM:
THE GENRE
OF
NATURAL
HISTORY

THE QUESTION of what to call Thoreau is a worrisome one, and has
its roots in his own persistent refusal to adopt any title. The position of being continually outside any accepted "profession" or genre is
precisely where he wished to place himself, although he may have, as
the occasion warranted, laid temporary claim to a title. Thoreau's
friend and first biographer, William Ellery Channing, felt he could
best summarize Thoreau's work and character by calling him a "poet-
naturalist"—using the word *poet,* of course, in the Transcendental,
rather than in its more restricted modern sense.[1] The first half of this
epithet has of late been dealt with with some seriousness, although it is
hard to argue with Walter Harding's judgment that "Thoreau can
hardly be called a major poet."[2] But Thoreau as *naturalist* has undergone a considerable, and largely negative, revaluation since Channing's
biography; though the question has not, I believe, been sufficiently
discussed in terms of natural history as a *literary* form.

Thoreau's natural history has often been attacked, as we have seen,
on the score of professionalism. One form of this charge can be summarized by the statement that Thoreau was no scientist at all because
he was always too literary.[3] Underlying, and somewhat preceding,
that line of argument, is the idea that Thoreau was simply a bad
observer, and that as a result his "naturalism" was inaccurate and can
be dismissed. James Russell Lowell, in his famous account of "renewing my recollection of Mr. Thoreau's writings" in 1865, insists that
Thoreau "was not by nature an observer" and goes on to argue that he
perceived only late, if at all, phenomena "familiar to most country
boys."[4] John Burroughs, in a somewhat later evaluation of Thoreau,

develops the argument more fully. Overall, Burroughs states, "when we regard Thoreau simply as an observer or as a natural historian, there have been better, though few so industrious and persistent." He goes on to expand upon that rather faint praise: "What he saw in this field everybody may see who looks; it is patent. He had not the detective eye of the great naturalist; he did not catch the clews and hints dropped here and there, the quick, flashing movements, the shy but significant gestures by which new facts are disclosed, mainly because he was not looking for them . . . He was more intent on the natural history of his own thought than on that of the bird. To the last, his ornithology was not quite sure, not quite trustworthy."[5] Burroughs documents his case by recounting some of the more egregious ornithological mistakes to be found in the *Journal*.[6]

As is so often the case, the standard of reference in Burroughs' essay is Gilbert White. Burroughs, himself a self-announced and respected naturalist writer, and an acknowledged disciple of Thoreau, sees White as a true naturalist, able to love "Nature for her own sake, or the bird and the flower for their own sakes, or with an unmixed and disinterested love."[7] As a result of Thoreau's lack of "disinterestedness," Thoreau's value to science, Burroughs says, is small. But this is offset by Thoreau's powers of description: "I trust I do not in the least undervalue Thoreau's natural history notes; I only wish there were more of them. What makes them so valuble and charming is his rare descriptive powers . . . If there is little or no felicitous seeing in Thoreau, there is felicitous description; he does not see what another would not, but he describes what he sees as few others can."[8] This emphasis on the naturalist as describer, rather than as seer or scientist, is, as we will see, an important sign of Burroughs' own, later, place in the development of the genre of natural history writing.

The brunt of the charge seems widely accepted, although there are modern rebuttals.[9] However, the emphasis placed upon the question of accuracy has allowed Thoreau's critics to miss an important point. Oddly enough, the inaccuracies to be found in that most exemplary of naturalists, Gilbert White, are customarily taken as signs of charm, or at most as vagaries to be justified, explained, and defended.[10] In any case, we have latterly come to expect the pace of discovery to be so rapid as to make most scientific writing of more than, say, ten years' age to be to some degree inaccurate. I think it is too easy to dismiss Thoreau's seriousness as a scientist; but in any case, it is important to realize that, when he played naturalist, he was undertaking a task in which writing and science were not at odds but rather inextricably mixed.

Burroughs seems closer to the essential point when, in a later reconsideration of Thoreau, he attempts to define Thoreau's uniqueness:

> Thoreau was not a great philosopher, he was not a great naturalist, he was not a great poet, but as a nature-writer and an original character he is unique in our literature . . . There are crudities in his writings that make the conscientious literary craftsman shudder; there are mistakes of observation that make the serious naturalist wonder; and there is often an expression of contempt for his fellow countrymen, and the rest of mankind, and their aims in life, that makes the judicious grieve. But at his best there is a gay symbolism, a felicity of description, and a freshness of observation that delight all readers.[11]

One can only imagine the degree to which Thoreau would have rejoiced to know that he had made the conscientious shudder and the judicious grieve; the signs of late-century gentility of the sort attacked by Santayana stand out in Burroughs' criticism. Yet Burroughs is, in the end, a defender of Thoreau; and he understands at least that it is as a writer — if not as a craftsman — that Thoreau is to be judged.

Burroughs' term — *nature-writer* — represents another attempt to find a usable and useful label for Thoreau; and it is no more immediately satisfying than any other label. The term carries with it a dismissive note to the modern ear; but it should not be so diminishing a term as it appears to be. It has the value, at least, of pointing us toward a large, if often apparently subliterary, body of writing, a continuously lively (and still living) genre of which Burroughs himself is an important practitioner.[12] That genre was, especially in the period from about 1790 to 1850, commonly called natural history — a term which at that point named a science, a methodology, and a kind of writing.[13] It is in the last sense that I will now use it, and seek to provide a general description of that sort of writing and of Thoreau's place within the genre.

My intention here is to show, briefly, in what ways natural history provides for Thoreau a literary tradition in which to place himself, one which allows and even encourages him to follow his inclinations and at the same time permits him to make himself an original, creative, and dominant writer.[14] What I propose depends in its turn on a pattern of what we might call *literary reassurance.* By this I mean the principle that writers, at crucial stages in their careers, seek out a tradition to fit into or, failing that, construct for themselves a tradition by linking apparently dissimilar writers and by redefining as seriously "literary" kinds of writing that are customarily considered non- or subliterary.

We have heard much in recent years about the anxiety of influence. Warner Berthoff has recently raised the question of whether those "models" of "the crisis of development and change . . . according to which younger writers more or less inevitably labor under the crippling burden of the great narrative past" apply at all well to American writers at work since 1945. He suggests that one weakness of these models is the presumption that younger writers struggle "to become creators of equal strength and *in the same performative mode*" (the italics are his). Berthoff goes on to demonstrate that the recent literary history of this country more commonly produces instances of the writer abandoning the "ruling mode" in favor of the effort "to maintain himself in whatever intentional sphere he can tolerate belonging to."[15]

The same process can be found to be at work among American writers before 1945. Indeed, it is arguable that such attempts to sidestep the burden of the past are a continuing characteristic of the American effort to establish a "native" literature not hidden in the shadow of foreign and more aged literatures. For a writer of Thoreau's time, in particular, the definition of a "ruling mode" was a difficult one, there being relatively little which could be said to constitute a live native literary tradition, and most of what did exist tending to fall, not within the great modes of poetry and narrative, but into such relative backwaters as the lecture, the essay, and the sermon.[16] It is perhaps this lack of a clear "ruling mode" which lends to some of the greatest works of American letters, especially during the American Renaissance, their range—or, to put it more negatively, their lack of formal definition. And that peculiarity is especially noticeable in Thoreau. We can, with relative ease, call *Moby Dick* a novel; but what are we to call *Walden?*

I propose to call it a work of natural history and mean more than that it is somehow "about" a pond and a loon. The term should, although it now usually does not, call to mind a substantial body of writing. Much of that writing has sunk into obscurity—not, perhaps, with any great loss in terms of aesthetic quality. But it would not have been so obscure to Thoreau. E. D. H. Johnson argues that "the treatment of natural history as a branch of literature is a long-standing tradition among the English,"[17] which may help explain the fact that Gilbert White currently enjoys a much more substantial reputation in England than in America, where a similarly serious treatment of natural history as literature does not seem to exist. But we recall how automatically Emerson, Burroughs, and so many other nineteenth-century American writers could refer to White, a sign, I think, of the fact that the divergence between England and America in this regard has not always been so distinct.

In any case, the books of natural history are unquestionably there. When, in the 1920s, Max Meisel undertook the compilation of the literary and institutional remains of what he chose to call the "pioneer century" (1769–1865) of American natural history, he found enough to provide the substance of a thick volume in small print listing titles and authors alone.[18] Philip M. Hicks, in his critical study of the natural history essay, a book which has for nearly sixty years remained the standard work on the subject, confronted directly the central problem of what "may properly be considered as included by the term 'natural history essay.'" His solution was a restrictive one, which "eliminates from consideration the essay inspired merely by an aesthetic or sentimental delight in nature in general; the narrative of travel, where the observation is only incidental; and the sketch which is concerned solely with the description of scenery."[19] Sadly, this distinction excludes the bulk of such important works as William Bartram's *Travels* (of which Hicks considers only the introduction as relevant to his discussion) and all of Jefferson's *Notes on Virginia,* as well as the more clearly moralistic works in the genre; and it allows Hicks to devote major attention to Crevecoeur, whose work seems to include rather less natural history than Jefferson's, and considerably less than Bartram's.[20] Nevertheless Hicks has no trouble tracing a line of descent from such early visitors to the continent as Thomas Heriot and John Smith, through the Transcendentalists, to John Burroughs; an honorable and long-standing pedigree.

On a less specifically literary basis, William Smallwood has suggested the very active interest in natural history in such literary byways as children's books, dating back to the *Bay Psalm Book.* At the same time he considers the degree to which travel books and correspondence are fundamental parts of the literature of natural history.[21] It is, in fact, the range and *inclusiveness* of natural history writing that are its most apparent characteristics. The early nineteenth-century American doctor, naturalist, and educator Benjamin Waterhouse proudly defined natural history as "a *nomen generalissimum:* a term comprehending a cluster of sciences, and a grand aggregate of knowledge."[22] We might paraphrase Waterhouse to make the point that, as literture, natural history is a grand aggregate of forms and manners. This range, especially in that it clearly includes local history, antiquarianism, travel literature, and field notes, makes the genre an especially tolerable intentional sphere for Thoreau. When, in "The Succession of Forest Trees," he claimed "a naturalist's liberty," we may suspect he had more in mind than simply permission to walk across his neighbor's pasture (*Excursions,* 185).

We need not, however, allow the literature of natural history to remain so vaguely defined as to include everything. E. D. H. Johnson attacks the problem first by delineating those assumptions which underly the writing of natural history: "that the study of nature is intellectually rewarding; that it is spiritually edifying; and that it is aesthetically gratifying."[23] Whatever this approach may sacrifice in terms of rigor, it has the great advantage over Hicks of including those elements of spirituality and aesthetics which are obviously in evidence, not only in Thoreau but in almost all substantial writers in the genre, and especially in the works of Hick's great exemplar, John Burroughs.

Johnson goes on to describe the "out-door naturalist" in terms which, while they explicitly refer only to English writers, seem especially applicable to Thoreau: "Without being recluses, these writers were by and large unworldly and sufficiently at odds with the temper of their times to dislike and resolutely avoid city life . . . Many . . . felt ill-at-ease under domestic or social constraint. Love of solitude bred among them a strong sense of individuality, nurtured, indeed, eccentricities and oddities of behavior."[24] The writing produced by these eccentricities displays the methodological presumptions we have already noted, especially a preference for first-hand observation and a concern with animate nature. The result, Johnson says, is a constant effort to "capture and portray the living drama of the natural world in all its vibrant inter-relatedness."[25]

We may, then, use three rough guidelines for the definition of the form: the principle of inclusiveness—the refusal, that is, to turn away from any source of information or any mode of discourse; the centrality of personal observation; and the clear attachment to place. Most often, the organizational principle of works of natural history is topographical or geographical. This may amount to a persistent attention to one locality—Selborne, Grasmere, or Walden. In the case of travel books, close attention is obviously paid to a sequence of places; but still, all of the informaiton is assembled and recorded as it arises from the nature of the locality. Even works such as Alexander Wilson's *American Ornithology* (1808–1814), which is primarily an illustrated catalogue, show the inclusiveness and sense of place characteristic of less schematically organized works. A modern critic has observed that Wilson's book soon "became a book not just about the birds of America but about the people, customs, economics, geography and social customs."[26] The context which allows this range of observation is that of habitat; the avenue of approach by which the writer may safely generalize is the observation of the nature of a particular place.

It may seem an obvious point—how is one to observe nature without doing it in some locality? But it is a fundamental distinction between the writing of natural history and the more modern modes of writing science, which tend not only to be more specialized but more abstracted from place, and more reliant on the observation to be done in a laboratory. The disappearance of place from much scientific writing is a sign of a reorientation of science and a revision of the underlying assumptions on which scientific study is based. Modern experimental science depends upon the control and limitation of context; the scientist constructs an experiment with a defined number and sort of variables, knowing that he is simplifying nature. In one sense this is directly related to the careful attentiveness which is at the heart of natural history; the natural historian, too, wishes to focus his attention, to simplify, to see detail. But he can do so only *within* a context, as that context is actually observable, and not in some artificial and limited recreation in laboratory or museum. Nature to the natural historian is an inextricably interrelated and interacting body, and to deny that interrelatedness in any way is to betray the nature of nature.

The matter can be carried one step further. To the natural historian nothing exists except in an environment, a place. This is as true of the self as it is of the sparrow. To follow the old injunction to know thyself is thus inevitably, to the natural historian, a task involving the investigation of the place where he is. The danger of solipsism is clear; the reading of nature as a reflection of the self can easily be a misreading. But to the natural historian—Romantic or pre-Romantic—there is really no choice but to risk the danger. The only alternative would be as pointless as observing stuffed birds in order to understand the migration of the sparrow. It is a point about which natural historians later in the nineteenth century began to feel very defensive. Rather than abandon this principle, the naturalist usually abandons the name of scientist, and along with it the respect which is more and more commonly accorded that name. "Interested as I am in all branches of natural science, and great as my debt to these things, yet I suppose my interest in nature is not strictly a scientific one," John Burroughs felt compelled to explain. "I seldom, for instance, go into a natural history museum without feeling as if I were attending a funeral."[27]

Beyond this unwavering belief that nature must be observed *in situ* and *in toto*—which is too often misinterpreted, especially in Thoreau's case, as eccentric willfulness or parochial chauvinism—the genre is most clearly characterized by what Johnson calls an "informal ease only to be found where there was no original intention to publish."[28] A great deal of English natural history writing occurs either in private journals or in personal correspondence, and there is little evidence to suggest, for instance, that Gilbert White began his correspondence with any eye toward eventual publication. But I have already tried to show that this informality is, even in Gilbert White, not altogether naive. The close connection between natural history writing as a genre and the most informal and personal modes of writing is undeniable; and it is clearly relevant to Thoreau, whose major late work may well be his journal. Thoreau, as is well known, was urged to "journalism" by Transcendentalism generally and Emerson in particular; but again, the prevailing tendency of natural history writing serves to legitimize that direction. And it is important to acknowledge, since we now know how serious a writer Thoreau was, that the informality of natural history writing is often, in part, an artifice. As we have seen, no matter for what reason he began his correspondence, Gilbert White did in the end produce a book and introduced it by writing more "letters" which were never intended to be correspondence at all, but rather to be introductory chapters.

The guise of amateur is an easy and effective one. Related to it is a certain apologetic tone in much natural history writing, an explicit refusal to claim the attention due to, and to abide by the standards expected of, "serious" literature—in much the same way, although not always with the same jocular intent, as Mark Twain's famous introductory injunction in *Huckleberry Finn*. Thoreau objected to this apologetic strain: "I have observed that many English naturalists have a pitiful habit of speaking of their proper pursuit as a sort of trifling or waste of time—a mere interruption to more important employments and 'severer studies'—for which they must ask pardon of the reader" (*"Huckleberries,"* 213). But he was equally capable of adopting at least part of that manner, if only as a joke. We recall his apparent apology as he begins *Walden,* and his oddly deprecatory presentation of Walden Pond itself (*Walden,* 3 and 175); and we will shortly see how he chose to begin "The Succession of Forest Trees." If there are examples of naturalists who were very nearly forced to write for publication, there are many more who, like Thoreau, adopt the protective coloration of the literary amateur.[29]

Much of our definition thus far has been derived from both English and American examples. There are elements of American natural history writing which seem peculiarly national.[30] One is its very strong nativist bias, understandable perhaps in a literature so devoted to place. The roots of this nativism lie not only in the general problem of American self-definition and its effects on the assertive tone of many forms of American expression, by which Dickens and almost all other foreign visitors were amused or offended. In natural history, the aggressive Americanness of the genre arises also from a particular controversy over the quality of American nature. The great French naturalist Buffon had included in his *Histoire naturelle, générale et particulière* the argument that the environment of America was such that no form of natural life could emerge there which would be equivalent to that found in Europe; America was biologically and irrevocably inferior. Understandably, American writers found this argument unacceptable, and set out to correct it.[31] Buffon thus provided what might not have been necessary: a spur within scientific circles to participate in the more general assertion of American pride. The challenge having been accepted, the nativism of American natural history writing becomes a part of the larger task. But it is worth remembering that the notion that the most blessed spot on earth might be a small pond in the vicinity of Concord rests in part on the prevailing tendency of science.[32]

A final element of American natural history is its utilitarianism. Again, the tendency extends well back in time. Philip Hicks quotes John Smith's *Map of Virginia,* which presents itself as being concerned with "such things as are natural in Virginia, and how they use them."[33] The element of *use* recurs in Bartram's *Travels,* where the author promises "useful observations."[34] The problem of usefulness had become, by Thoreau's time, a troublesome one for naturalists. Hicks finds in Bartram's *Travels* "a shifting of the emphasis from the utilitarian to the aesthetic and philosophic viewpoints."[35] If so, the shift is hardly a conclusive one. The importance of the useful—the hoeing of beans, for instance—continues to be an important validating strain in most natural history writing. But increasingly the definition of *use* moves away from the more strictly material and economic. More and more commonly, natural history writers are moved to write because they see too much use being made of nature, and use of the wrong kind. It is a keynote of *Walden,* of course, but Thoreau had encountered the same note elsewhere, as we will see when we consider William Howitt's *Book of the Seasons,* one of Thoreau's particular favorites.

Natural history writing can thus be described as informal, inclusive, intensely local, experiential, eccentric, nativist, and utilitarian, yet in the end concerned not only with fact but with fundamental spiritual and aesthetic truths. Within this genre Thoreau seems to have chosen to place himself; and it is clearly an appropriate home, serving to support those habits of mind and style which are the elements of Thoreau's uniqueness as a writer. And, to return briefly to the issue of the anxiety of influence, the peculiarly low esteem with which the genre as a whole was regarded (and largely continues to be regarded) as *literature* may have constituted an additional source of appeal to a writer who desired above all to be original. Individual writers of natural history, most notably the ubiquitous Gilbert White, were highly esteemed; but more as representative men than as writers. The standard term of commendation for White is charm; and that charm seems to depend in its turn on his not being considered a writer at all. Thoreau's earliest defenders often felt compelled to explain his roughness as a writer, or to assert the seriousness of his literary intentions.[36] The lack of immediate awareness by Thoreau's early readers that he was unequivocally an artist may be taken as a sign of the extent to which he had successfully adopted the mannerisms of the genre.

And by placing himself in this tradition, he successfully avoids the problem of battling with great precursors. There are in the history of natural history great scientists (Linnaeus and Buffon), saintly figures (Gilbert White), and great men (Thomas Jefferson); but not, by the standards of the time, great writers. Thoreau thus adopts an "intentional sphere" that allows him the freedom to undertake a wholly original literary task: the elevation of a subliterature into high art.

WE CAN ESTABLISH a base line for the precise relation of Thoreau to the genre of natural history by considering his late lecture "The Succession of Forest Trees." The circumstances of its composition, for presentation to and eventual publication by the Middlesex Agricultural Society, serve in part to explain its peculiarly "scientific" manner. Certainly it is, in comparison with Thoreau's greater works, orderly in an unusually explicit way. After a short introduction, to which we will return later, Thoreau presents that "purely scientific subject" which engages his attention. This setting of the question is remarkably direct while at the same time recognizably Thoreauvian in its combination of off-handedness and self-assertion: "I have often been asked, as many of you have been, if I could tell how it happened that when a pine wood was cut down an oak one commonly sprang up, and *vice versa*. To which I have answered, and now answer, that I can tell, — that it is no mystery to me. As I am not aware that this has been clearly shown by any one, I shall lay the more stress on this point. Let me lead you back into your wood-lots again" (*Excursions,* 185–186). As in so many of Gilbert White's letters, the solution (and Thoreau allows no doubt that there *is* a solution, near at hand) begins with the observation of an apparently mysterious yet commonplace phenomenon. Although the lecture attempts to propound a general hypothesis, it has its feet solidly grounded in the local. Returning to the woodlots is not only a rhetorical venture; again and again as the lecture proceeds, Thoreau will turn for supportive evidence to his own researches in the vicinity of Concord. He will as well feel free to draw upon other information — lessons recorded, for instance, in "Loudon's 'Arboretum' " (*Excursions,* 193 and 200). But it becomes increasingly clear that such "foreign" evidence is only corroborative, and not altogether reliable, while that derived from Thoreau's parochial strolls and plantings (buttressed with a show of dates and numbers that might please a more modern experimentalist) is the fundamental source of the solution of the mystery. There is no question in Thoreau's mind about the solubility of at least this one of Nature's mysteries, and no question but that the careful observation of what is immediately at hand can, in the end, produce explanations applicable more generally. The task Thoreau sets himself is demonstration, not speculation; to see and to think is to understand.

Having committed himself to a specific problem and having promised a careful demonstration of the answer, Thoreau takes the necessary preliminary step of analysis and definition. The issue, as he sees it, is twofold. He first considers the question of propagation and, by the application of a Yankee version of Occam's razor, decides that "of the various ways by which trees are *known* to be propagated—by transplanting, cuttings, and the like" it is clear that the "only supposable one under these circumstances" is seed (*Excursions*, 186). The real problem then, is not one of propagation but (and this is his second point) a question of transportation: "It remains, then, only to show how the seed is transported from where it grows to where it is planted. This is done chiefly by the agency of the wind, water, and animals. The lighter seeds, as those of pines and maples, are transported chiefly by wind and water; the heavier, as acorns and nuts, by animals (p. 186)."

As I have argued elsewhere, the customary direction of Thoreau's considerations of nature is toward complication, confusion, paradox, and myth. The assumption has been made, by Lowell, Burroughs, and many others, that this was in effect a fault of his mind; he had not the detective eye and therefore could not help but see complication. But in this lecture we can watch Thoreau carefully and effectively *simplifying*, and doing so by the most orderly of mental and rhetorical steps, logic (if A, then B) and careful definition ("It remains *only* to show . . ."). Like any good scientist, he has chosen his ground and laid out his method in advance; and he is ready, like a good debater, to shift the burden of proof to his opponent, should any appear: "No tree has ever been known to spring from anything else. If any one asserts that it sprang from something else, or from nothing, the burden of proof lies with him" (p. 186). The issue does hold one added complication, and one which will allow Thoreau to be more Transcendental: the problem of "vitality," the possibility of seed remaining potent during the time needed to transport it. But the bulk of the lecture is what we might expect: an assembling of evidence demonstrating how seed may be transported in such a way as to allow oak to replace pine in cut-over land.

Thoreau of course does not abandon altogether his normal habits of style. He misses no opportunity to make jokes at the expense of the postal service and the Patent Office, and thereby to show the superiority of natural over human modes of transport (*Excursions,* 186–187 and 194). But he is unusually restrained—perhaps to prove that he can be, and certainly in a way which ought to warn his readers that his relative lack of restraint elsewhere (his willingness, for instance, to suggest that Walden Pond may have sprung from something uncommon or from nothing) is not the whim of a sloppy thinker but the intentional device of a careful naturalist.

Thoreau never, in the present case, altogether willingly diverges from his own experience; he provides a more than adequate summary of the lecture in the sentence "I will state some of the ways in which, according to my observation, such forests are planted and raised" (*Excursions,* 187). "According to my observation" is not a polite phrase; it is a brief statement of method. The assembling of evidence, however, is never the most lively of undertakings, and the lecture as a whole is far from the most readable of Thoreau's works. The price of rigor seems to be a loss of the characteristic knottiness to be found in an essay like "Wild Apples," dating from roughly the same time. Thoreau does, however, have an eye out for the larger issue. He remarks, for instance, on the degree to which man's reliance on his own supposed ingenuity is, in the end, uneconomical: "So, when we experiment in planting forests, we find ourselves at last doing as Nature does. Would it not be well to consult with Nature in the outset? for she is the most extensive and experienced planter of us all, not excepting the Dukes of Athol" (pp. 197–198). But even here Thoreau toes the evidentiary line he has set; for this aside is, on one level, no more than a largely worded reaffirmation of the fundamental operative principle of the talk: *Observe.*

The wariness with which Thoreau approaches second-hand evidence is also reminiscent of Gilbert White. When Thoreau cites the great eighteenth-century American naturalist William Bartram (*Excursions,* 199), it is only to affirm what he himself has already observed. Indeed, the arrangement of the paragraph goes somewhat beyond this;

Thoreau's data is presented as confirming Bartram, and not the other way around. The authority, therefore, is something requiring experimental support, and not an unquestioned source of evidentiary data. More often than not Thoreau finds his second-hand information either incorrect in some way, or simply (and unnecessarily) repetitious of what might be obtained more directly. As he observes of English planters who experiment with the propagation of trees, too many men "appear not to have discovered that [their method] was discovered before" (p. 194). That prime discoverer is, of course, not man at all, but nature. To emphasize the point, Thoreau turns immediately from the English experiments to the local woodlots, recounting what he observes as he "walks amid hickories, even in August." The more reliable bits of supportive second-hand evidence are not those assembled by the experts at all, but by those who, like Thoreau, walk and observe, like the "sportsman" whom Thoreau encounters on an October stroll (p. 195).[37]

Secondary evidence, then, if useful at all, can only be corroborative. The risks involved in relying overmuch on the reports of others are driven home when, in considering the question of the vitality of seed, Thoreau cites, within the space of a few pages, "Loudon's 'Arboretum'", the Massachusetts state naturalist George B. Emerson, stories from ancient Egypt, and the reports of "several men of science" as to the growth of beach plums in Maine (*Excursions*, 200–201). The presence, in this catalog of authorities, of Egyptian folktale is at first surprising, although as we have seen the writer of natural history seeks his information from a wide pool of sources, and we know well that Thoreau has a fondness for old myths, especially those with some metaphoric or Transcendental application. The effect of the presence of the Egyptian tales is, however, quietly deflating to the pretensions of the scientists. For all their rigor and experimentation they can still be lumped together with the hoariest of legends—company they would, no doubt, find highly uncomfortable. And as it turns out, the men of science are no more accurate or reliable than the story-tellers; all rest their arguments on such shaky or invisible grounds as to be useless. Thoreau, on the other hand, is always sure of his ground. He believes that seeds can "retain their vitality for centuries under favorable circumstances" (p. 201). That is partly a mystic belief, a commitment to the mystery of seed. But as science it is based not on credulity but on walking the ground first hand, prowling the site of a house standing "on land belonging to John Winthrop, the first governor of Massachusetts," where he discovers, long-buried but still vibrant, the signs of a wealth of plant life "not found before" in his perambulations. The point is confirmed by Thoreau's attempt to grow yellow squash from seed sent to him—the joke re-emerges—by the Patent Office (pp. 201–203).

We may begin to realize by this late stage of the lecture how consistently the experts whom Thoreau finds inadequate turn out to be foreign, and particularly British. There is a strong element of American pride involved in his ending the essay with John Winthrop and with the life story of the "premium" squash in the most recent Middlesex County Fair, after he has completely undercut the reputation of poor Loudon. The image of the seed arising from the ruins of John Winthrop's house has vast symbolic possibilities, as does the squash whose progeny will, he believes, spread to distant places "where no hound ever found it before" (*Excursions,* 203). But the possibilities are in this case left undeveloped, although the subtle critic may want to suggest that Thoreau, very quietly, refights the Revolution by arraying America and France (the two homes of the squash) against Britain.

There is a peroration, and one which moves in a characteristic direction; but it is oddly short-winded, as if the occasion or the restraining demands of a more rigorously "scientific" approach have left Thoreau no energy to pursue his larger interests. Robert Sattelmeyer remarks that, in fighting his "kind of rear-guard or guerilla action against scientific materialism," Thoreau "dispels . . . myth in order to call attention to a more fundamental and real mystery."[38] That formula applies well to very nearly all of Thoreau's work, and the intention in this lecture is explicit. The larger mystery is that of the seed—"I have great faith in a seed" (*Excursions,* 203). And the sign of that mystery is a vision of American abundance—"the corner of my garden is an inexhaustible treasure chest" (p. 204). That vision is available to any farm boy, did he not, even as the Concordians in *Walden* seem to, "love darkness rather than light" (p. 204).

IT IS CLEAR then that even so late in his career, Thoreau retained a sufficient grasp on the fundamentals of the genre so that he could write a straightforward and "scientific" natural history essay, with all of the expected earmarks: inclusiveness (from the woods of Concord to the lore of ancient Egypt, and from squash to the Patent Office); fundamental localism; insistent reliance on direct observation *in vivo;* native pride; practicality (his knowledge will produce—or allow to be produced—better forests *and* better squash); and, finally, moral observation. The desire, apparent if only schematically at the end of the lecture, to extend the observation of the phenomena of Nature into a larger context of spiritual concern is by no means a departure from the norm. Indeed, as may be evident from E. D. H. Johnson's description of the natural history writer, cited above, the sense that observation of nature is inherently a spiritual and moral enterprise seems to have been, at least up to Thoreau's time, a universal assumption, and one seen as in no way in conflict with the necessary tasks of science. In America, which, as Norman Foerster has put it, "meant chiefly nature," this tendency to moralize is especially strong.[39]

One of Thoreau's own favorites among natural history books, the Englishman William Howitt's *Book of the Seasons,* shows clearly the commonly accepted conflation of fact and uplift. Howitt proposes to move month by month through the year in the hope of doing "something which shall tend to the prosperity of [my] country and [my] species."[40] The organizational principle which Howitt employs, that of the agricultural calendar (we might today call it an almanac), allows him to go beyond the most apparent meanings of "prosperity." Indeed, he is very much concerned to counteract the more materialistic interest in prosperity which he feels is induced by "the calculating spirit of trade" (*Howitt,* xiv)—a phrase which shows Howitt to be a rough contemporary of Carlyle and influenced by the great Romantics. Howitt describes his own work thus:

> My plan has been to furnish an original article on the general appearance of Nature in each month, drawn entirely from my own regular observations through many seasons; and finally, to superadd a great variety of facts from the best sources, as well as such as occurred to myself after the principal article was written. To these, a complete table of the Migrations of Birds; a copious list of Garden Plants which come into flower in the month; a Botanical Calendar, including a select number of the most beautiful or interesting British plants, and an Entomological Catalogue of about three hundred of the most common or remarkable insects; a notice of Rural Occupations, and, finally, one of Angling, are added. (*Howitt,* vi)

If we recall the various sorts of writing to be found in White's *Selborne,* we will recognize them again here, with perhaps a more explicit intention. In any case, here is inclusiveness with a vengeance, and usefulness inextricably mixed with moral improvement, the latter often in the form of citations from literature and Scripture, with which Howitt introduces each month but which he leaves out of his general description of the work as a whole.

Howitt thought of "a Book of the Seasons" as a "*beau idéal*" (*Howitt*, v). Thoreau, in his turn, thought Howitt's book an ideal middle ground, "neither too scientific, nor too abounding in technical terms and phrases to be comprehended by the general reader, nor yet of too miscellaneous and catch-penny a stamp for the would-be literati or blue-stockings" (*Early Essays*, 26). The mature Thoreau found himself drawing together his "own regular observations through many seasons," so we need not think that his affection for Howitt and Howitt's method was only the enthusiasm of his youth. A Calendar in particular, and natural history writing in general, might allow Thoreau the moralist and Thoreau the observer to coexist.

But in "The Succession of Forest Trees" the coexistence seems rather stale and unprofitable; Thoreau's effort to work up his science into symbol at the end of the lecture, however characteristic, simply does not rise, rhetorically, in the way that the last pages of *Walden* might lead us to expect. Whatever its virtues as science, the lecture as art is something of a disappointment; and it may well be a disappointment that Thoreau himself shared. At any rate he assembled, in his last years, the elements of a larger work, which he called "Dispersion of Seeds" and which grows, quite literally, from portions of his published lecture.[41] Despite its size—nearly four hundred manuscript pages— the work is unfinished and fragmentary; but a look at it and its apparent (and even more fragmentary) companion piece, "Notes on Fruits," as well as at the reconstructed essay "Huckleberries" and the late nature essays which Thoreau lived to complete, may help us understand more fully the ways in which Thoreau hoped to exploit and to reform the writing of natural history.

SCHOOLING
THE EYE
AND HAND:
THE LATE
NATURAL HISTORY
ESSAYS

U NTIL ABOUT a decade ago, it was customary to lament the sad
decline of Thoreau's last years—a legend apparently fostered by
Thoreau's editors.[1] In part the misconception seems to rest on a lack of
attention to Thoreau's usual method and pace of writing. It took him
nearly eight years to recast his excursion of 1839 into *A Week on the
Concord and Merrimack Rivers,* the book he completed while living at
Walden Pond. The experience at Walden did not become an account
in the form which satisfied the author until another nine years had
passed. After the completion of *Walden* Thoreau had only some eight
years to live, and not all of them, by any means, in sound health and
full energy. Yet he managed to see into print major portions of *The
Maine Woods* and *Cape Cod* and to put into finished form "Walking,"
"Wild Apples," and "Autumnal Tints," as well as the political
writings on John Brown and "Life Without Principle." And that is
only the visible evidence, much of it available to us only through the
mediation—and, alas, the meddling—of Thoreau's literary executors.
The evidence of the manuscripts which Thoreau left at his death is
even more conclusive.[2]

It is the sheer bulk of this material, and the meticulousness with
which Thoreau compiled it—especially those tables and indexes that
he culled from his journal—which make it hard to credit the idea that
Thoreau's intellectual energies were somehow on the wane after
Walden. And the particular kind of work he was often doing in these
years helps establish all the more clearly Thoreau's continuing devo-
tion to natural history as method and as genre. What shape these
efforts might have taken, had Thoreau been granted that "longevity"

which, as Emerson lamented, was required by "the scale on which his studies proceeded,"[3] is of course a matter of supposition. It now seems probable that neither the "Calendar" which Sherman Paul assumed was in progress nor the "book on the Indians" which F. B. Sanborn suggested, was the goal that Thoreau had in mind.[4] Those things which we have, both published and unpublished, from Thoreau's last years make it seem that Thoreau may, in his own way, have been at work on something not unlike that "Natural History of Concord" which his friends so often and wistfully proposed as a suitable work for his maturity.

CERTAINLY "Dispersion of Seeds," Thoreau's complete reworking of "The Succession of Forest Trees," might quite easily be organized on the model of White's *Selborne.* The kinds of writing we found there — collection, catalog, "monography," and essay — are equally easy to identify in Thoreau's manuscript. Of catalog there is, as in *Selborne,* a relative lack, although Thoreau does at one point compile a list of "aboriginal" and "European" plants within the range of his observation ("Seeds," 233). And there is catalog of a type more to Thoreau's taste in the listing — almost an annotated bibliography — of the most relevant and useful sources on the problem of "succession" (pp. 239–243).[5] The fruit of the cataloger's and classifier's work is apparent too in the consistency with which Thoreau uses the Linnaean nomenclature. In an effort, as he says in the "Notes on Fruits," to "make distinctions — & call things by their right names" ("Fruits," 4), he takes care to label and describe each of the plants he takes up. We should not expect Thoreau to be wholly satisfied with any "borrowed" system of naming; and indeed he is as fond of the common as of the scientific names. By the end of "Dispersion of Seeds," he is emboldened to establish his own classification — that of "New woods" — as a way of approaching the underlying scientific question to which the manuscript and the lecture which preceded it are addressed ("Seeds," 366).

But however much the work relies on classification and "distinction," "Dispersion of Seeds" is no catalog. The bulk of it is taken up by observation, accumulated in the vicinity of Concord by the most painstaking fieldwork. Thoreau's data are often presented in a rather more orderly manner than Gilbert White's; there is nothing, really, to compare to the nearly random collection of phenomena we found in

White's thirty-ninth letter to Thomas Pennant.[6] What seems, in part, to have provoked Thoreau to revise his lecture is the sense that, however adeptly he had solved the mystery "that . . . is no mystery to me" (*Excursions,* 185; "Seeds," 244), there remained much more to be said about those observations that had led to his confident answer. In "The Succession of Forest Trees" he restricts himself, for instance, primarily to the pine and the oak; in "Dispersion of Seeds" he ranges through the hemlock, the larch, the cherry, red cedar, tupelo, ash, apple, pear, birch, alder, maple, elm, willow, and poplar — not to mention plants well outside the category of trees, including the dandelion, the thistle, and even the huckleberry. In the lecture, the red squirrel figures prominently as an agent of the transportation of seed; in "Dispersion of Seeds," the squirrel is very nearly the hero (as man is quite clearly the villain), appearing at least fourteen times and twice occupying as much as ten pages of continuous text.[7] So great is Thoreau's fascination with the squirrel's work that he is moved to remark upon the precedence of the animal's instinct over man's "reason" ("Seeds," 20v) and even — with quite comical results — tries, unsuccessfully, to emulate the squirrel as a gatherer of pine-cones ("Seeds," 39r–41r).

Part of the organizational problem which Thoreau faced — and which he did not live to solve — is that the range and amount of his observation simply cannot be contained within the conceptual framework of the original lecture. The change in title is significant, for it had become apparent to Thoreau that the problem of "succession" — which he felt he had solved — was really only a part of a larger process by which seeds generally are dispersed, and by which, more mysteriously, "we find ourselves in a world that is already planted, but is also still being planted" ("Seeds," 225). That mystery, in turn, takes him toward the still larger one of the seed itself, in which, as he had announced at the end of his lecture, he had "great faith" (*Excursions,* 203) and which evokes from him moments both of wonder ("Seeds," 191–192) and of calculation, as when he attempts, whether comically or metaphysically, to determine the precise size of the seed of the earth (p. 67).

Gilbert White too had found himself moved toward explanation by the act of arraying facts; but the facts which Thoreau finds simply will not lie still so readily as those that fill the earlier letters in *Selborne.* Gilbert White had, in the end, been willing to undertake monography and even (but only very late and rather hesitantly) to move toward reflection and interpretation. To Thoreau, the monograph—the organized essay on a single topic—was central, as all of his completed late essays show, and as appears in "Dispersion of Seeds" in his effort, early on, to organize his work by species ("Seeds," 7–27r and 27r–41r). But the greater goal, and the one with which his manuscript begins, is the effort to understand fully and even to preach:

> We are so accustomed to see another forest spring up immediately as a matter of course when one is cut down, whether from the stump or from the seed, never troubling ourselves about the succession, that we hardly associate seeds with trees, & do not anticipate the time when this regular succession will cease, & we shall be obliged to plant, as they do in all old countries. The planters of Europe must therefore have a very different & much more correct notion of the value of seeds than we . . .
>
> As time elapses & the resources from which our forests have been supplied fail, we too shall of necessity be more & more convinced of the significance of seed.   ("Seeds," 6)

That we may need to learn from Europe is a surprising argument to find in a work derived from "The Succession of Forest Trees," which as we have seen is so carefully contrived to assert the predominance of the native over the foreign, whether it be in science or in squash. It is however a point Thoreau repeats at the end of the manuscript, when he remarks how Europeans have "taken great pains to learn how to create forests." By contrast, our less diligent and less informed American approach has left us with "poor pastures and poor forests" ("Seeds," 397). The prize is not altogether to be granted to old countries of course; Europeans may know better than Americans but squirrels know better than Europeans (*Excursions,* 193; "Seeds," 285). But that makes all the clearer Thoreau's concern for our decaying condition and his eye for the coming day when, like Adam, we find ourselves no longer in an ever-renewing garden but compelled, and perhaps too late, to live by the effort of our own planting. It is extinction which worries him, as when he notices the loss of chestnut, hickory, and oak through the "decay of soil": "The time will soon come, if it has not already—when we shall have to take special pains" ("Seeds," 274).

The seed will save us—but only if we learn its "significance." Toward the teaching of that significance Thoreau turns his manuscript.

It is worth noticing what may indeed be obvious—that Thoreau is simply not writing for the same audience as were Gilbert White and Darwin. The difference is not only, and indeed not primarily, geographical and chronological. White, we recall, had addressed his letters to "thinking minds" of equal talent as observers and with an equal interest in observing; the presumption is that writer and reader share an understanding of how the world operates and a desire to develop a more detailed sense of that operation. Thoreau, quite evidently, writes with no such presumption. His readers are not Thomas Pennant and Daines Barrington, exchanging their own "autopsia" for his. Thoreau sees about him a world of the obtuse, of farmers who, foolishly trying to derive one last meagre rye crop from a pasture, destroy a valuable birch forest ("Seeds," 90–91), of "proprietors" who are maddeningly, and madly, "blind to [their] own interest" (p. 387), of travelers who fail utterly to notice what is around them (pp. 31r–32v and 281). Even those who go out more appreciatively into nature may fail, if they do not first learn how to look: "Such is the difference between looking for a thing, & waiting for it to attract your attention. In the last case you are not interested at all about it, and probably will never see it" (p. 281). White had of course noticed an abundance of misconception and bad science; but in the end he writes as the reader's colleague. Thoreau writes as a schoolmaster, and one much more given to discipline than that young Thoreau who would not cane his students.

In the task of what he calls elsewhere "the schooling of [the] eye and hand" (*Excursions,* 287), Thoreau depends again on the method of the natural historian. Much of his observation serves to establish his own credentials. He demonstrates to us, to an almost bewildering degree, his familiarity with the "authorities."[8] And he provides us with set-pieces of good science, as when he investigates the puzzling discovery of caches of pitch-pine twigs ("Seeds," 14–17). His methodology is sound. First he records the phenomenon, having watched and waited long enough to be certain that it is not merely an accident: "I notice every fall, especially about the middle of October, a great many pitch-pine twigs or plumes, which have evidently been gnawed off & left under the trees . . . It is plainly the work of Squirrels. As I had not chanced to detect their object, I resolved last fall to look into the matter." The assumption he makes is that nature, however mystical, is also purposeful, that she functions, as scientists propose, according to elemental and comprehensible laws:

> Anything so universal and regular, observed wherever the larger squir-
> rels and pitch-pines are to be found, cannot be the result of accident or
> freak, but must be connected with the necessities of the animal . . .
> The squirrels used only food and shelter. I never see these twigs used in
> constructing their nests, hence I presume that their motive was to ob-
> tain food . . . My swift conclusion was, that they cut off these twigs in
> order to come at the cones, & also to make them more portable.

That the conclusion, once the problem has been correctly framed,
comes swiftly does not disguise the fact that it is based on years of
observation; nor does it allow Thoreau to forgo the task of testing his
hypothesis by observing once more. This he promptly does, with the
happy result that his "theory was confirmed." Nor does the matter
stop there, since he can further corroborate his theory by turning to
the results of the fieldwork of others, even those living near him in
benighted Concord, where "my neighbor" provides the final piece of
confirmation.

Thoreau repeats the method twice more, each time attacking a new
problem ("Seeds," 292–294 and 324–327); and he shows himself to be
as able an experimenter as he is an observer, by nurturing a willow
seed so as better to understand the process of the tree's germination
(pp. 183–184). The quality of that experimental work, and Thoreau's
confidence in his own capacity as a scientist, are quietly confirmed
when he finds Darwin making a not dissimilar experiment to establish
the fecundity of pond mud (p. 226). But the point of this naturalizing
is not to prove Thoreau's superiority to us, his readers; rather, he
would show us the ready and easy way. Thoreau presents himself as a
better observer than the mass of men, but not because of some mystical transformation. He has simply trained himself. That is why the
neighbor enters into the science, as elsewhere do an old hunter (p.
44v), several "sportsmen" (pp. 279–280), a trapper (p. 336), and a
variety of other neighbors (pp. 69, 318–319, 335), several of whom
also appear in "The Succession of Forest Trees." Unlike the sad John
Field of *Walden,* Thoreau's neighbors in this work *can* see, if not
always quite well enough.

Thoreau himself, on the other hand, is not quite so correct as he has
been elsewhere. There are, he is careful to point out, some problems
which, unlike the caches of pine twigs, he has not yet solved ("Seeds,"
265–266 and 314–317). From time to time Thoreau is not able to test

out his "suppositions" in the field; and he distinguishes those things he "suspects" from those things he has observed (p. 374). It is not that any specific problem is somehow insoluble, although in the largest sense, the wonder of seed may indeed be just that. But usually the reason for unfinished business making its way into "Dispersion of Seeds" is that the work is to include both completed science and science in process; Thoreau is a model to us not only of the convinced naturalist but of the proper impulses of the naturalist who finds himself still in some doubt. Thus, when he admits that his effort to understand oak seedlings is not yet complete, he follows that admission with a page or so of his subsequent examination of the data (pp. 296–297). On the whole, he is self-reliant enough — and perhaps skeptical enough of the skill of his fellow beings — to be unwilling to leave the investigation to others, as Gilbert White often does; as we might expect, he prefers to go over the ground for himself.

It is no surprise to find Thoreau less self-effacing than White, less willing merely to be one of those blossomless pioneers of whom he speaks in "The Natural History of Massachusetts" (*Excursions,* 130). But he is more self-effacing than the Thoreau of other works. We will have occasion to consider the point again when we look at the late nature essays which he lived to complete; here I will simply record the impression that the "I" which we encounter in "Dispersion of Seeds" is both less dominant and strikingly less difficult than the "I" of, say, *Walden.* It is essential to Thoreau's pedagogical point that he demonstrate, not how little his readers know in comparison to him, but how much. Repeatedly he begins his observations on common ground. Of pitch-pine he says, "All my readers probably are acquainted with its rigid conical fruit, scarcely to be plucked without a knife" ("Seeds," 7); and again, only a few pages later, "All have noticed . . . dense groves of pitch-pine" (p. 10). The same note begins his treatment of the white pine (p. 27), and as the piece continues, the reader is readily and easily identified as the one who has seen or will see: "you will often see" (p. 146); "if you dig up old oak stumps . . . you will commonly find" (p. 332); "the squirrel which you see at this season" (p. 4); "how commonly you see" (p. 370); "look under a nut tree . . . and see" (p. 322). The moment of true observation, however common, is frequently cast in the conditional or placed syntactically in the future, as a sign that the reader must still be trained; but the repeated emphasis, not on the chosen few or the eccentric individual, but on the reader generally, demonstrates Thoreau's faith that even in these latter days a widespread reform of the eye and thus of the soul is possible.

Thoreau teaches most effectively by example, both of what we fail to see at the moment and also of the ways in which we may look more profitably and understand more fully. His manuscript is, as he tells us, an effort to recast his own experience in a more comprehensible order: "I do not always state the facts exactly in the order in which they were observed but select out of my numerous observations extended over a series of years the most important ones & describe them in a natural order" ("Seeds," 244). The natural order seems, finally, to have escaped him; the manuscript remains unformed. But in terms of establishing the method of observation which will produce the desired results, Thoreau manages a number of clear demonstrations.

His intention is not only to have us learn what he knows, but also to learn how to learn; and he is confident enough in his own abilities as teacher to set problems for us to solve. At one point, finding in a woodlot near Concord evidence of the process of development which is his prime concern, and which, as he has often reminded us, too many travelers, farmers, proprietors fail to see, he remarks that "there are many such problems in forest geometry to be solved" ("Seeds," 386). That fact is, by this stage of the manuscript, no news to us; nor is it unusual that Thoreau goes on to lay out one such problem for us: a grove of pine and oak has, he believes, grown up around an old and now invisible wall. The surprise comes at the end of his observations, which take up nearly a page and include a diagrammatic sketch: "Given these facts — to find the wall. If you think a moment — you will know without my telling you, that it is between the large pine wood & the oak" (p. 386). It is the schooltext turned to Transcendental purposes — our qualifying exam, if you will, which he presumes we can easily pass. He is still a little ahead of us — he goes on, not just to solve the geometry of the woodlot, but to read from that geometry the "history" of the woods for some fifteen years prior to the moment he shows us. It is just such a reading of history, and by no means an uncritical one, that he insists we must do, for practical as well as metaphysical reasons: "Our wood-lots of course have a history & we may often recover it for a hundred years back, though we *do* not . . . Yet if we attended more to the history of our woodlots, we should manage them more wisely" (p. 385).

Here, then, is a past which must be present to us, if we are to survive into the future:

> The history of the woodlot is often . . . a history of cross purposes—of steady and consistent endeavor on the part of Nature—of interference & blundering with a glimmer of intelligence at the 11th hour on the part of the proprietor. The latter often treats his woodlot as a certain Irishman, I heard of, drove a horse—i.e. by standing before him & beating him in the face all the way across a field.
>
> What shall we say to that management that halts between two courses? Does neither this nor that but botches both? I see many a pasture over which the pitch or white pine are spreading, where the bushwhack is from time to time used with a show of vigor—I despair of my trees (I say *mine*, for the owner evidently does not mean that they shall be his) & yet this questionable work is so poorly done, that those very fields grow steadily greener & more forest-like from year to year, in spite of cows & bush whack, til at length the farmer gives up the contest, from sheer weariness, & finds himself the owner of a woodlot (which he does not deserve). ("Seeds," 396)

The passage is a useful precis of the concern of the whole of "Dispersion of Seeds" and of the mood, of some despair, which recurs within it. Yet still there is the "glimmer of intelligence" even on the part of the last of the lost, the proprietor; and how much more of a glimmer in those for whom Thoreau designs his teaching? What "we" shall say, and do, about mismanagement (and the pronoun is both the we of prophetic sermon and the we of commonality and fellowship) depends in large part upon how effective that teaching is.

THE HISTORY which Thoreau sees, and which he would have us see as well, is a history of change, of a sort not so unquestionably hopeful as the regenerative force of spring which is the climax of *Walden*. The dispersion of seeds is a phenomenon of fall and of winter, although it is as well both a result of and a prophecy of spring: "And for this these silken streamers have been perfecting themselves all summer—snugly packed in this light chest—a perfect adaptation to this end—a prophecy not only of the fall—but of the future springs. Who could believe in prophecies of Daniel or of Nathan that the world would end this summer, while one milkweed with faith matured its seeds?" ("Seeds," 214–215). Thoreau shares with the milkweed a faith in seed; but it is not in this manuscript a faith which is commonly so reassuring.

Explicitly, he is convinced that there is at work "a steady progress according to existing laws" ("Seeds," 33r). It is to the discovery and definition of a "developmental theory" (p. 225) that "The Succession of Forest Trees" is specifically devoted, and this is a major concern of "Dispersion of Seeds" as well. But on closer and more immediate observation, the "progress" is not always so distinct. There is, in fact, a struggle being played out before us, reminiscent of that at the edge of Walden Pond (*Walden,* 181–182). The adversaries now are not land and water, but man and nature. There is no doubt where Thoreau stands in the matter; nature is "persistent" and "vital" ("Seeds," 270), while man is, all too characteristically, dull and inobservant. Indeed, nature is so much the better cultivator that our best course would be to concede the struggle to her: "By a judicious letting Nature alone merely, we might recover our chestnut wood in the course of a century" (p. 283). A more careful attention to the economy of nature would, in the end, be more economical in man's terms as well.

That this happy result may be in some doubt is, first of all, a measure of the obstinate interference of man the farmer and proprietor. One of the most frequently repeated moments in "Dispersion of Seeds" is that moment when man fails to see what is occurring around him: "For many years the daily traveller along these roads nay the proprietor himself, does not notice, that there are any pines coming up here, & still less does he consider whence they came" ("Seeds," 31r–32v). Since the process continues even without the traveler's attention, there is something to be said for this state of ignorance, at least when compared to man's more obstructive role: "These which we see springing up thus in distant and neglected meadows & by fences show what would happen over all the intervening space if it were not for our cultivation—that there is nothing to prevent their springing up all over the village in a few years, but our plows & spades & scythes" (p. 31r). Even in the midst of Main Street, the seed prevails, in the form of a white birch growing in the gutter (p. 147); and Thoreau reads the same lesson in the example of a single pitch-pine which grows in his yard (p. 13).

There is, in fact, something at times quite chilling in the fecundity of Nature, which, if not checked in some way, might literally overwhelm the world ("Seeds," 202), as the fecundity of ponds defeats all man's efforts to clear them of lilies (p. 227) and as imported plants observed by Darwin utterly drive out the native growth (p. 234).

There is perhaps a hint of that Nature without reference to man which Thoreau saw atop Ktaadn:

> The consequence of all this activity of the animals—& of the elements in transporting seeds is that almost every part of the earth's surface is filled with seeds or vivacious roots of seedlings of various kinds—in some cases probably seeds are dug up far below the surface which still retain their vitality—the very earth it is a granary . . . so that to some . . . its surface is regarded as the cuticle of one great living creature—
> Nature so fills the soil with seeds, that I notice where travellers have turned off the road & made a new track for a short distance, the intermediate narrow & bare space is soon clothed with a little grove which just fills it. (p. 338a)

Living on this skin of nature, man is little more than a parasite, and one whose occasional efforts to strike a new course serve only to show how easily nature might obliterate all human traces. Still, man—the obtuse wanderer—has a part to play. Elsewhere in the manuscript Thoreau notices that even "the most ragged and idle loafer or beggar, may be of some use in the economy of Nature, if he will only keep moving" and thus distribute the seeds which stick to his coat (p. 232). It is, we might add, one of the few times in which civilization seems to present a natural advantage—since "civilized man transports more of these seeds than the savage does" (p. 232).

The processes in which Thoreau is interested here, we should remind ourselves, are not cyclical but successive, not the reappearance, seasonally, of certain plants but the replacement of one plant by another; and there is, if never quite explicitly, the notion in "Dispersion of Seeds" that man might be one part of the economy which is in its dotage. Certainly the smallest phenomena carry an apocalyptic weight, to the informed observer: "[The pitch-pine seedling] was, as it were, a little green star with many rays half an inch in diameter, lifted an inch and a half above the ground on a slender stem. What a feeble beginning for so long-lived a tree! By the next year it will be a star of greater magnitude, and in a few years, if not disturbed, these seedlings will alter the face of nature here. How ominous the presence of these moss-like stars to the grass—heralding its doom!" ("Seeds," 11r). The moment nicely plays off the scientist, with his eye for measurement, against the prophet, who knows his Scripture well enough to realize that "all flesh is grass."[9]

It is the inevitability of these processes which makes man's efforts when he "interferes with this renovation" ("Seeds," 243) so silly. Indeed man is himself part of the process, whether by carrying seeds on his coat or by cutting and burning the pasture and forest, so that the next plant may succeed to its place. Yet there is the contradictory note, which we saw at the very beginning of "Dispersion of Seeds," in the suggestion that this new and ever renewing land is somehow growing old, and that the efforts of man are, against all probability, succeeding, although hardly with the result which man expects. This sense of decay and loss underlies the urgency of Thoreau's desire to educate us as naturalists: "Now it is important that the owners of these woodlots should know what is going on there & treat them & the squirrels accordingly. They little dream of it at present. They appreciate only some very gross results. They have never considered what is the future history of what they call their wood lots. They have designs of their own on those acres, but they have not considered what Nature's design is" (pp. 282b–283). It is the learning of that design—and the acquiescence to it—which might, in the course of a century, bring back the lost forests of Concord.

How to teach is, as we have seen, not a question which presents any great difficulty to Thoreau; the methods of the natural historian are available, and he seems convinced they will serve his purpose. The problem, however, of finding a "natural order" that will properly reflect both his literary purposes and the character of the processes which he hopes to describe—that, it seems, was in the end insoluble. He begins the manuscript seeming to move species by species through the major trees; but such a scheme misses that part of the dispersion process which involves the sequence from tree to tree in the history of woodlot or pasture. He spends long pages arraying those agents which disperse the seeds, most notably the squirrel and that unwitting agent, man; but to focus on the individual agent misrepresents the case too, since in nature Thoreau constantly sees interactive processes. Agents work, not in isolation, but as part of an economy, as when both wind and water cooperate to spread the willow ("Seeds," 173–174). Even the distinction between fruit and seed, upon which his two large uncompleted projects are based, is in a fundamental way wrong, although he tries, with regard to fruits, to defend the separation ("Fruits," 421–423). He knows that fruit and seed are inextricably joined, in the scientific facts of the case; which is why huckleberries figure in both "Dispersion of Seeds" and "Notes on Fruits" and why he spends so much time in the former manuscript talking of the acorn, which is, botanically, not a seed but a fruit.

His efforts to cull the journal are organized largely by month and season, and that organization carries over, at least in part, to these manuscripts. We have observed that "Dispersion of Seeds" is primarily concerned with fall and winter; so "Notes on Fruits" begins, chronologically, in early summer, and not very happily so:

> The middle of June is past and it is dry & hazy weather. We are getting deeper into the mists of earth, we live in a grosser element, further from heaven these days, methinks. Even the birds sing with less vigor & vivacity. The season of hope & promise is passed, and already the season of *small fruits* has arrived. We are a little saddened because we begin to see the interval between our hopes & their fulfillment. The prospect of the heavens is taken away by the haze and we are presented with a few small berries. ("Fruits," 587; emphasis Thoreau's)

In that fallen condition, the cycle of the seasons is, as in *Walden,* a comfort; and "Notes on Fruits" might well, had Thoreau lived, kept the sort of organization by chronology, taking up plants in the order in which they bear fruit, which much of the manuscript now has. "Notes on Fruits" is presented as a kind of guidebook, but one no less vitally necessary than the more complex instruction of "Dispersion of Seeds":

> I think that a wise and independent, self-reliant man, will have a complete list of the edibles to be found in a primitive country in his waistcoat pocket at least, to say nothing of matches & warm clothing, so that he can commence a systematic search for them without loss of time . . . Why a truly prudent man will carry such a list as the above in his mind, at least, even though he walk through Broadway or Quincy Market . . .
>
> Accordingly I have been taking an account of stock in good season. ("Fruits," 424, 592)

Of that guidebook we have, in anything like coherent form, only the "chapter" on huckleberries, to which we shall turn in a moment. But we should not be led away too soon from "Dispersion of Seeds." However well "an account . . . in good season" may work as an organizing principle for Thoreau's list of fruits, it will not serve for an essay devoted to "development." There, although the dispersion undergoes a crucial stage at one particular season, the important cycle is not that of the year but that of at least the century. The proprietor who fails to see the woodlot being born in his pasture will not live to realize his error; it is his heir who will derive the benefit ("Seeds," 31r–32v).

Thus in talking of the "history" of forests, neither the season, so useful in *Walden* and potentially so useful in "Notes on Fruits," nor the self, which is such a prominent presence in all Thoreau's earlier works, will suffice as a metaphor for the natural order; neither is long or capacious enough to organize Thoreau's data fully. We will have occasion shortly to consider how Thoreau attempts, in his finished late essays, to move away from, or perhaps beyond, the dominating self of his earlier works. At the same time he has largely abandoned his other common principle of organization, the excursion. The "walk" is by no means altogether missing in these late works; but there is nothing to compare to the fundamental geography, the essential movement toward and away from a place, which underlay Thoreau's account of his trip on the Merrimack or his time at Walden or his trips to Maine or Truro or Wachusett. "Dispersion of Seeds" was, apparently, to be a book written about and even for farmers and proprietors, not saunterers of a wide-ranging sort.

It presents no great difficulty for Thoreau to say these things, here and elsewhere: that fruit and seed are in fact one; that plants succeed one another in a long but (as he hopes) progressive sequence, a sequence so extended in time that the experience of the individual cannot adequately encompass it; that the agency by which this process occurs is complex and interactive; that no travel is worthwhile unless the eye be trained first, and that no travel is necessary once the eye has been trained. But those "facts" seem to deny him the kinds of literary order which are, at first glance, most apparent in his material and which had been most congenial to him in the past. One solution to the dilemma is to abandon altogether any larger organization in favor of the shorter and more easily defined essay; what that answer offered by way of relief we will consider in a moment. But such a solution is, in its way, a surrender, an admission that the effort to express that economy (or, to use its more modern etymological cousin, ecology) which is fundamental to nature is beyond Thoreau's capacity. Another solution, but one no more satisfying on this score, would have been to compile a natural history of a more traditional, and hence less organized, sort, a "collection of autopsia" similar to Gilbert White's. Such a compilation would have involved abandoning precisely what Thoreau seems to have hoped to do with and to the natural history essay as he found it — to bring to it a sense of large and literary *form* which had been notably absent. By his own lights, to have written only a "Natural History of Concord" might well have represented the saddest of failures.

THOSE LATE nature essays which we have in more finished form[10] share with "Dispersion of Seeds" and "Notes on Fruits" a sense of the lateness of the hour: "But ah we have fallen on evil days!" ("Huckleberries," 248) But they share as well, in varying degrees, an intention to teach, and a belief that the lessons to be learned are near at hand and — to the prepared eye — none too difficult to perceive: "Only look at what is to be seen, and you will have garden enough, without deepening the soil in your yard. We have only to elevate our view a little, to see the whole forest as a garden" (*Excursions,* 172). The result will not only be useful practically, as a better knowledge of edibles would be to a wanderer lost on Broadway; it will also be a moral and spiritual elevation, escaping the curse of Adam and keeping alive the spirit of the place: "Let us try to keep the new world new" ("Huckleberries," 254).

It seems at times that the requisite observation calls for a kind of arcane learning, "of Indian knowledge acquired by a secret tradition" ("Fruits," 585). Indeed, his search for the truly wild crabapple, that "half-fabulous tree," takes Thoreau to the geographic limit of his sauntering, St. Anthony's Falls on the Mississippi (*Excursions,* 301 – 302). But the "special province" of "Wild Apples" is not that *Malus coronaria,* any more than it is those cultivated *Mali urbaniores* which Thoreau dismisses earlier in the piece. Thoreau's true concern is the apple which, having escaped cultivation, grows even so near at hand as "a rocky tract called the Easterbrooks Country in my neighborhood" (*Excursions,* 299), barely two miles from Concord Center and perhaps three-and-a-half miles from Walden Pond.[11]

Each of the essays begins unequivocally within the world we all know. One point of the array of Scripture and authority at the beginning of "Wild Apples" is, after all, to show that man has always known apples — making the apple, rather sadly, the "most civilized of

all trees" (p. 292). Thoreau introduces the huckleberry thus: "I presume that every one of my audience knows what a huckleberry is—has
seen a huckleberry—gathered a huckleberry—nay tasted a huckleberry
—and that being the case, that you will not be averse to revisiting the
huckleberry field in imagination this evening" ("Huckleberries," 212).
And even "Autumnal Tints," which opens with a discussion of how
often the "brilliancy of our autumnal foliage" has been overlooked,
especially in literature (*Excursions,* 249), starts its actual work with an
item of mutual observation: "By the twentieth of August, everywhere
in woods and swamps we are reminded of the fall, both by the richly
spotted sarsparilla leaves and brakes, and the withering and blackened
skunk-cabbage and hellebore, and, by the riverside, the already blackened pontederia" (*Excursions,* 252). That "we" has its limits—Thoreau
will speak of things which drivers, owners, town-fathers, selectmen,
Puritans, and farmers know not; but "we" may be reassured about
how easy our task is to be, when we learn that children, madwomen,
and all walkers commonly share the knowledge Thoreau has to offer
us.[12] If Thoreau is, here and elsewhere, somewhat in advance of us,
the reason has nothing to do with the secret initiations he may have
undergone; it is simply that, as he tells us, "I have learned to look" (p.
318). Thoreau is our model of the man who has trained himself: "You
would not suppose that there was any fruit left there, on the first
survey, but you must look according to system. Those which lie ex-
posed are quite brown and rotten now, or perchance a few still show
one blooming cheek here and there amid the wet leaves. Nevertheless,
with experienced eyes, I explore amid the bare alders" (*Excursions,* 317;
cf. "Huckleberries," 243). We might fairly summarize a major concern of these essays as being the question of how to "look according to
system."

   Each of the essays undertakes this by proceeding from something we
all know, to that which Thoreau knows (but which we could easily
see for ourselves), to that which we seem not to know at all, but must
learn if the final and irremediable fall is to be forestalled. The naturalist
knows better than most how essential it is to begin with what we
have ourselves observed; for it is only those personal observations
which we can, in the end, trust as a measure of what we are offered by
way of "accounts." One cannot truly "visit" the fields in imagination;
one must, quite literally, have walked the ground personally. The
essays contain the expected examples of the limitations of "authority."

The most notable case is the lamentable town history of Boxboro ("Huckleberries," 257–259), but flaws are apparent even in better works, like that of the naturalist Michaux, who overlooks the red maple in favor of its less spectacularly colored cousin, the sugar maple (*Excursions,* 261). Those warnings should, to a degree, make us wary of Thoreau's own authority—all the more so when he recounts his misadventures in a leaf-covered swamp (p. 266) or when he admits that he too had for "so many Augusts" failed to notice the purple grasses (p. 257). We must also take note of the cautionary tale of Dr. Manassah Cutler, native and botanist much like Thoreau, who nonetheless has his vision so "led astray by reading English books" that he "lightly" dismisses the wondrous huckleberry ("Huckleberries," 225–226).

Thoreau's repeated admonition is not to believe him, and certainly not to believe unquestioningly in any account. His own renderings are, as he reminds us in "Autumnal Tints," only "some extracts from my notes" and not that true book which would have been an exact copy of nature, without any words at all (*Excursions,* 251). What he wants us to do is look for ourselves; and he is sure that such looking will have its result: "If you look closely you will find blueberry and huckleberry bushes under your feet" ("Huckleberries," 227). Or, again: "When you come to observe faithfully the changes of each humblest plant, you find that each has, sooner or later, its peculiar autumnal tint" (*Excursions,* 289). Or, of the complex process by which the semicivilized apple grows: "Now, if you have watched the progress of a particular shrub, you will see that it is no longer a simple pyramid or cone, but that out of its apex there rises a sprig or two, growing more lustily perchance than an orchard-tree" (*Excursions,* 305).

Thoreau is clearly distrustful of science; but his warnings are, if not outweighed, then at least balanced by a reliance on the work of scientists. If in "Wild Apples" the tree of knowledge is omitted from one catalog ("Fruits and Fruit Trees of America"), it can be found in the works of two of Thoreau's standard references, Loudon and Evelyn (*Excursions,* 309–311). If Thoreau in "Autumnal Tints" finds the botanist likely to miss "the grandest pasture oaks," the warning follows by only a few sentences his acknowledgment of the value of his own "botanical rambles" (*Excursions,* 286). And when he proceeds, in that same work, to seek examples of proper sight, models for "him who shoots at beauty," he includes a fisherman, a berry-picking girl, a hawk — and an astronomer (p. 288). "Huckleberries" includes an explicit defense of the work, if not of the diffident literary manner, of the naturalists. Despite their mistaken, or perhaps hypocritical apologies, Thoreau insists that "all mankind have depended on them for this intellectual food," to be found in their attention to facts of nature no larger and yet no less important than those berries which are his own subject, and which will have the triple effect of feeding body, intellect, and spirit ("Huckleberries," 213).

His wariness about science arises because he knows, as he argues at some length in "Autumnal Tints" (*Excursions,* 284–288), that any single way of looking will cause us to miss something. But if we conclude from his remark about "How differently the poet and the naturalist look at objects!" (p. 286) that he is implicitly on the side of the former, we have forgotten that the essay began by showing us how completely a not-inconsiderable poet has failed to see the very phenomena the essay extolls (p. 249). In any case he cannot suppress the habits of the scientist: "I suspect that some scarlet oak leaves surpass those of all other oaks in the rich and wild beauty of their outlines. I judge from an acquaintance with twelve species, and from drawings I have seen of many others" (p. 278). The point he is trying to make is not really a scientific one at all; but a poet would not need to be so careful to distinguish what he knows from what he only suspects, nor would he need to recite his sources, even briefly, by type and number. Thoreau is not shy either about employing the technical terminology of botany — "Autumnal Tints" is full of "culm" and "panicle" — or about recommending the use of the microscope as a way of improving our knowledge of the huckleberry ("Huckleberries," 216). Most centrally, perhaps, he relies on that great work of naming which had been the fundamental contribution of the eighteenth century to the sciences. He is careful to give us the scientific name — as well as native names which are our own, or better still the Indians' — of each plant he examines. He is aware of the false diplomacy of scientific naming which leaves the huckleberry named after a French chemist who may well never have seen the fruit (p. 214); but he is equally aware that the scientific names can convey essential truth, as when he examines the etymology of *Phytolacca decandra,* the poke (*Excursions,* 253–254). Naming is to Thoreau always a complex and transcendent task; and these names are at least a place to start, a common if not always steady ground.

Science, as he says, can often do no more than reassert the fact (*Excursions*, 250); but that is, often, exactly his own intention. Certainly careful scientific description is generally the point from which he sets out toward the larger and more prophetic truth he seeks. We will see the same device at work in *Walden*, where the natural history of ponds helps us understand more fully the mythic history of one pond. Among these essays, the test-case is "Wild Apples," which is, as I will argue again shortly, the least unequivocally scientific of all, because the most thoroughly mythic. But we remember he begins that essay with a geologist and with history; and the apple itself is introduced as if in a textbook:

> The apple tree (*Pyrus malus*) belongs chiefly to the northern temperate zone. Loudon says that "it grows spontaneously in every part of Europe except the frigid zone, and throughout Western Asia, China, and Japan." We have also two or three varieties of the apple indigenous in North America. The cultivated apple tree was first introduced into this country by the earliest settlers, and is thought to do as well or better here than anywhere else. Probably some of the varieties which are now cultivated were first introduced into Britain by the Romans. (*Excursions*, 292)

That the "facts" of the matter happen, if only quietly, to serve his parabolic purposes is of course why he has chosen to play scientist. He will indeed discuss "two or three varieties" of apple; and spontaneous growth serves in part to identify the apple tree with the Tree of Knowledge which grew without seed, and also to emphasize the primal hardiness of the tree, even in its half-cultivated state. The history of the tree in America establishes this world's fecundity; the history of the tree in Britain leads us back into mythological times, especially if we recall the pseudo-history of Roman Britain which identifies the founder as the descendant of Aeneas. Thoreau's use of science as the grounding of myth does not, however, reduce its accuracy as science; such is the food which the naturalist can provide even to the parabolist.

For all that he rebukes the obsequiousness of the old naturalists, even less to his taste is the more arrogant science which loses sight of the fact that it serves as means, not end; or a science that would pretend to be unattainable to those of us, however amateur, who are willing to learn. Thoreau proposes no experiment we cannot re-create, undertakes no observation we cannot make just as well ourselves.

Even his discovery of the wild apple is something we might duplicate, were we willing to ride the "cars" far enough West. Indeed, the fundamental acts which Thoreau prescribes, like the plucking and tasting of the apple, we *must* do ourselves, since no description is adequate and no farmer is capable, Thoreau insists, of picking the fruit for us without damage (*Excursions,* 297; "Huckleberries," 249).

We feel, and quite justly, that the central character in most of Thoreau's longer works is Thoreau himself; but it is arguable that the central consciousness in these essays is not "I" but "you" or "we." Certainly the first-person pronoun is infrequent, relatively speaking, and often tied directly to the second and third person. "I" occurs, for example, only three times in the first six paragraphs of "Autumnal Tints" and then is swept aside by a flood of "we" and "our" — nine of them in the seventh paragraph (*Excursions,* 249–251). It is ten paragraphs along in "Wild Apples" before the first "I" appears, and then it is in the rather unobtrusive formulation "I learn from Loudon" (p. 291). The "I" is somewhat more prevalent early in "Huckleberries," particularly if we include the epigraph.[13] But of the four appearances of "I" in the first five paragraphs of that essay, two present Thoreau simply as observer ("I have noticed . . . I have observed") ("Huckleberries," 211–213). To establish some measure of the amount of change in Thoreau's manner, we need only remark on the first two paragraphs of *Walden,* where "I" appears, by my count, 19 times (*Walden,* 3–4); or the first two of *Cape Cod,* where "I" shows up nine times; or of "Ktaadn" which includes "I" six times.[14]

What may be even more significant is the way in which Thoreau verbally connects his own observations with ours. In "Autumnal Tints" he recalls his first encounter with the purple grasses:

> I saw, thirty or forty rods off, a stripe of purple half a dozen rods along, under the edge of the wood, where the ground sloped toward a meadow. It was as high-colored and interesting, though not quite so bright, as the patches of rhexia, being a darker purple, like a berry's stain laid on close and thick. On going to and examining it, I found it to be a kind of grass in bloom, hardly a foot high, with but a few green blades, and a fine spreading panicle of purple flowers, a shallow purplish mist trembling around me. Close at hand it appeared but a dull purple, and made little impression on the eye; it was even difficult to detect, and if you plucked a single plant, you were surprised to find how thin it was, and how little color it had. But viewed at a distance in

a favorable light, it was of a fine lively purple, flower-like, enriching
the earth. Such puny causes combine to produce these decided effects. I
was the more surprised and charmed because grass is commonly of a
sober and humble color. (*Excursions,* 252)

The passage is nicely representative of the manner of these essays, in its
preference for the observed fact over the personality of the observer
and in its willingness both to examine closely and to see from a
productive distance, to be if you will both scientist and sightseer. But
what I would emphasize just now is the way in which the "I" who is
seeing all of this disappears, first into the impersonal construction "impression on the eye" and then into that "you" who is, like Thoreau
himself, delightfully surprised. The transformation is perfectly acceptable colloquial usage; but it is also an open encouragement to us to
identify ourselves with the trained eye of Thoreau. That both he and
we are surprised, and that he chooses to recount at such length his *first*
encounter with the plant—which he must before that time have overlooked as often as we have—serves to diminish all the more the
distance between us and him. Thoreau is frequently surprised in these
essays; and is it unfair to find this wide-eyed onlooker so much more
accessible to us than the man who is so repeatedly and so intimidat-
ingly (not to say arrogantly) knowledgeable in *Walden?*[15]
   In any case the shift in language here from "I" to "you," from
Thoreau the trained eye to the readers whom he would train, re-enacts
rather closely the didactic and even prophetic point of these essays.
Thoreau provides us with an intermediary in the person of himself; an
intermediary who has, among other things, saved us the task of ran-
sacking the authorities for those points on which they are, relatively
speaking, reliable. And he acts out both the means and the end—both
the necessary kind of observation, capable of surprise, willing always
to examine, willing for that matter to walk again where he has walked
so many times before, and able to lay facts, whether first-hand or second-hand, fruitfully alongside one another; and also the happy condition which results from that observation, with both the belly and the
eye satisfied, with an appreciation of the ripeness of life and a capacity
to accept the imminence of death. We will have occasion very shortly
to discuss Thoreau the saint, and to find him still being a scientist. In
these essays his halo is less terribly visible, and both his humanity and
his science are all the more evident and all the more appealing.

THOREAU'S distrust of the world's professions is both wide and deep; and we should not be surprised to find him wary of science, as he is in these essays. But the critical argument that Thoreau becomes more antiscientific over time does not seem to fit the facts of these late writings especially well. He is still, this late in his life, trying to write natural history of a recognizable and traditional sort. Thoreau remains firmly attached to the methods of the naturalist, and to a belief in the redemptive value of the insight which those methods produce; it is for this reason that he can so readily offer us himself as a model for our own effort to become better walkers and thus better seers.

But it is equally true that all these late essays show how unwilling Thoreau was to adopt *in toto* the manner and aims of the natural history writer. He may, in "The Succession of Forest Trees," be writing science; but clearly in "Wild Apples" he is writing prophecy more than anything else. The effort on Thoreau's part to bring to natural history a sense of form and of myth, which he did not find in the genre down to his own time, is noticeable in the simple fact that we would mistake none of these essays for the work of Gilbert White. Even "The Succession of Forest Trees" displays a willingness to have scientific fact blossom into metaphor in a way that White would, in all probability, have rejected as a particularly dangerous form of analogizing.

To understand in somewhat more detail how Thoreau attempts to reform the natural history essay, it may be worth considering in what ways these essays, which share so much in terms of intention and manner, are unlike one another. Taking "The Succession of Forest Trees" as one pole—the extreme of traditional "pure science" to which Thoreau the mystic and individualist would allow himself to approach—we can set "Wild Apples" at the opposite pole. As we have seen, in "Succession" the choice and ordering of evidence is primarily determined by the scientific "mystery" that Thoreau sets out to unravel. The fact that the mystery is, to his eye, no mystery at all, allows Thoreau to demonstrate how susceptible Nature is to human understanding, properly schooled and properly grounded. And the character of the evidence, indeed the character of the very process he attempts to describe, allows him to move somewhat beyond the strict scientific line of his argument, into matters for example of national pride and into the symbolism of seed. But neither didacticism nor prophecy take him far from the science which is the announced work of the essay. In "Wild Apples," for all its show of authorities and nomenclature, we do not have to wait until the Scripture of the final page to realize that the determining principle is more the fable, the parable, the myth, than the science.

Neither "Autumnal Tints" nor "Huckleberries" strays so far from the kind of monography we saw in Gilbert White; but neither is satisfied, as White customarily is, to stick to the facts of the matter. In terms of organization, "Autumnal Tints" follows quite carefully the chronology of the season; and the somewhat more disorderly "Huckleberries" is at least unified in its focus on a single species and its near cousins. At first glance we have no trouble believing that "Autumnal Tints" is what Thoreau says it is: "some extracts from my notes" (*Excursions,* 251); and we know that this phrase describes quite precisely the genesis of "Huckleberries," which Thoreau left only partially extracted from those "Notes on Fruits" which were in their turn extracted from his field notes in the journal. Science and the scientist are continually present in each essay, and continually accurate, so far as Thoreau knows, and so far as any second-hand account can, in his view of things, be accurate. But one would at least have to say that this is a more meditative kind of science than is common in traditional natural history writing before Thoreau. What concerns Thoreau in the end is not a fact but how it corresponds to a condition of the observer; it is our response to fact that is central, and too often inadequate. Science is peculiarly able to assemble and to state the facts; and we could do much worse than be scientists. But science alone will not produce that "answering ripeness" which Thoreau seeks in himself and in us (*Excursions,* 263).

Thoreau's distance from science does become more marked as his despair grows, which again suggests that "Wild Apples" represents the polar opposite of the confidence of "The Succession of Forest Trees." Certainly huckleberries prove to be less an object of observation and more an example of the state of things as Thoreau moves toward that sense of the loss of "natural rights" and of the "true relation to nature" which proves to be the final subject of "Huckleberries" (pp. 249, 251). "Autumnal Tints," despite its recurrent awareness of death, is on the whole not an especially pessimistic piece; the syntactical confidence of its final words ("When you come to observe . . . you will find . . . ") represents quite adequately its mood. "Huckleberries" ends with a pun—perhaps the only pun Thoreau ever apolo-

gized for—and a sense of the separation of man from Nature: "Some
men think that they are not well in Spring or Summer or Autumn or
Winter, (if you will excuse the pun) it is only because they are not indeed *well*, that is fairly *in* those seasons" (p. 262). We are left uncertain
whether those "men" are redeemable, and whether they include "you"
or "us"; but we are reminded as well how conclusively *in* season the
central voice and even the reader of "Autumnal Tints" is placed. The
prophecy which ends "Wild Apples" is that the loss may well be per-
manent and universal; even "he who walks" will not be able to see, "a
century hence" (*Excursions,* 321).

In that despairing mood Thoreau turns the natural history essay
almost into self-parody. There is in "Wild Apples" a richness of
science, and of course of pseudo-science, which is, in its way, more
fully developed than in those essays which seem more willing to trust
science. Certainly the various modes of organization which we saw as
possibilities in "Dispersion of Seeds" are all used. Thoreau describes to
us in proper sequence the life cycle of the plant, from sprout (*Excursions,* 303) to that final fruition when Thoreau harvests from "old trees
that have been dying ever since I was a boy" (p. 309). That life cycle
(it includes no seed presumably because these trees grow spontaneously)
parallels, roughly, the progression of seasons from spring (p. 299)
to December, the day of the "frozen-thawed apple" (pp. 319–320).
And of course the larger progress—if that is the word—of all of
history is played out, from that moment "a short time previous to the
appearance of man on the globe" (p. 291) up to the present and even
beyond, into the apparently lamentable future (p. 321). The chronology is conveniently mythic, including that Garden where the Tree
of Knowledge first grew and the looming Apocalypse of extinction.
The myth does not, however, interfere with the scientific movement
of the essay through categorization and definition, beginning, in good
Linnaean form, with the "order of the *Rosaceae*" (p. 290), thence to
the apple itself, which (once more borrowing from good authority,
Pliny) he subdivides into wild and civilized (p. 292). That he is, he insists, less interested in the civilized, does not dissuade him from
describing them carefully (pp. 294–298) before moving on to his
"special province" of the wild, which he further subdivides into the
truly wild and the semicivilized (pp. 299–302), and then even further
in his catalog of names (pp. 315–317). Thoreau's manipulation of scientific Latin is robust and informed; and the catalog is both a skillful

parody and an explicit alternative to the work of the world's classifica-
tionists. He has warned us earlier that he has "no faith" in the workings of those "pomological gentlemen" who name apples (p. 310);
now he becomes one. He proposes his catalog as a "pleasant pastime";
but the essay makes it clear that the passing of time is an element of
the doom hastening upon us.

By the end of the essay the futility of its own science is apparent (pp.
321–322). To be a good observer will no longer do when there is
nothing to observe. Then, to know apples through "authority" or
imagination will no longer be susceptible of the vital test of personal
experience; and so by its own standards natural history will no longer
work. The fall which overtakes man and apple at the conclusion of
"Wild Apples" is not a season but an irreversible state, in which
science will be futile because it will have no data on which to work.
All we will then have to take the place of the redemptive act of observation is the inadequate and unreliable device of reminiscence.

THOREAU'S turn away from science—if that is what it is—is more a
comment on the state of the world than a recognition of any inadequacy in science. Toward the end of his life he is still writing essays
which, by their very titles and subjects, identify themselves as natural
history, and which at the same time try to expand the form into myth
and prophecy. Thoreau's place in the history of the genre of natural
history writing is a crucial one. His youthful praise of William Howitt
indicates his awareness, even as a young man, of the possible conflict
between scientist and writer, a conflict which he can in his essay on
The Book of the Seasons overcome by asserting the existence of a *via
media* (*Early Essays*, 26). But that conflict could not for long be so
easily and briefly laid to rest. The general course of development of the
genre can be seen, in a very abbreviated way, in the contrast between
the announced intention of White's *Selborne* and the subtitle of an
equally charming modern work, Lewis Thomas's *The Lives of a Cell.*[16]
White, we recall, intended to contribute to a larger body of knowledge, that "universal correct natural history" which it was the great
effort of his century to assemble. His attitude is modest, but his position as an amateur did not in his eyes debar him as a matter of course
from making valuable, albeit small, advances in areas we can still call
scientific. Thomas, by contrast—himself, we might observe, a fully ac-
credited *professional* of science—calls his book "Notes of a Biology

Watcher." He observes, not nature, but science itself; he observes, we might say, the observers and the observations. His task as a writer is not to add to scientific knowledge (which demands another and much more specialized mode of disclosure that must abound in technical and catch-penny terms) but to mediate between science and the commonality, to be an explicator, an interpreter. Moral observation—of which his book is full—is now distinctly a separate enterprise from science itself.

Nina Baym has persuasively documented what she interprets as Thoreau's increasing distrust of science, and his increasing preference for "old naturalists." But in 1860 Thoreau still unashamedly claimed for himself a scientific investigation, and a scientific result. He has, then, not yet conceded the inevitability and the unbridgeability of the gap between writing and science, between interpretation (in the broadest sense) and investigation. He is very probably the last important writer to be able to do so. His successor John Burroughs, by contrast, believes much more conclusively that his role is only that of mediator between an increasingly complex and specialized science and a general readership. The amount of writing Burroughs did on the interrelationship of science and literature[17] is in itself symptomatic of the fact that the battle is lost and all that remains is the task of drafting a new treaty to seal the defeat. Thoreau, then, stands at the moment when the differentiation between amateur and professional, between man of letters and man of science, becomes distinct and irrevocable; or, we might say, he stands just before that moment and makes a last effort to refuse to accept the split.[18]

The signs of that refusal are clearly evident in the introductory paragraphs of "The Succession of Forest Trees" (*Excursions,* 184–185). The pages represent an obvious effort by an experienced lecturer to put his audience at ease; but as is so often the case Thoreau is making a most serious point in an epigrammatic and apparently offhand way. The brunt of his introductory remarks can be summarized in his own question: "why choose a man to do plain work who is distinguished for his oddity?" The question arises from Thoreau's consideration of the "queer specimens of humanity" whom he looks forward to meeting again at the Cattle Show—especially those who at first seem wholly out of place and useless. The connection to his own case is clear when he insists that, odd though it may seem, "I have some title to speak to you to-day," even on a matter of science. He is careful, even while adopting his favorite guise as plain-talking Yankee, to remind the audience that his credentials are in order, as surveyor and as naturalist. He does not in the end apologize, as elsewhere he condemns English naturalists for doing. In fact he *refuses* to apologize. But it is clear that he knows he must offer at least an explanation and defense, an *apologia* if not an apology, of the notion that a Transcendentalist dare speak of science. In the history of the genre, that *apologia* would not have been so necessary a generation before; and it would not have been tenable a generation afterward.[19]

Precisely why this sea change in the accepted aims and permitted functions of natural history writing takes place in the middle of the last century is a question far beyond the scope of this study. Certainly it is related to the general shift from those sciences (botany, geology) directly concerned with description and classification to those (chemistry, physics) which rely on controlled experimentation. By maintaining his place out-of-doors, as he must, the natural history writer increasingly isolates himself from those indoor places where the cutting edge of scientific advance is nowadays to be found.[20] The natural historian remains an explorer, but he must increasingly define himself not as discoverer but as preserver, a force acting against the calculating spirit so much in evidence and against the scientific materialism which John Burroughs condemned so firmly and so often.

The ever-increasing sense that nature is under siege and that it is vital to try to preserve it in words is, in its turn, related to the broadest of cultural changes. Consider how easily James Russell Lowell could summon up as a standard of comparison the experience of "every farm boy"; and how certain he could be that a substantial portion of his own and Thoreau's readership had at least the continuing opportunity to see nature at first hand. Being a fact of American life at the time, this made Thoreau's irony especially heavy—that same farm boy enters the concluding paragraph of "The Succession of Forest Trees" and is never far out of sight in *Walden,* but he willfully refuses to see. It is, however, an assumption about the nature of the audience which only the most specialized of writers—for instance, the editor of some agricultural journal—could reasonably make today.

Thoreau's place in these developments is, in literary terms, pivotal. He is arguably the last major American writer to believe he could be both scientist (in some actual, nonmetaphorical sense) and a man of letters, at the same time and in the same work. The degree to which he has subsequently been attacked for being neither, and for foolishly sacrificing some larger success on this synthetic altar, for being too literary to be scientific or for being, in the late journal, so consumed by the minutiae of natural history as to deprive us of some supposed "After Walden," is a sign perhaps not so much of Thoreau's failure as of our own, of our place in a later day where the synthesis of art and fact which he continually set as an ideal for himself is no longer considered worthy or possible.

· 5 ·

NATURALIZING
EDEN:
SCIENCE
AND SAINTHOOD
IN *WALDEN*

T HE LATE ESSAYS of Thoreau demonstrate that he had not lost his
conviction that the methods of the scientist were both personally
congenial to him and of great use in the transcendent tasks he wished
to accomplish. Scholars who argue that one can, by viewing Thoreau's
work chronologically, see a growing negativism in his attitude toward
science, seem to miss his basic consistency. Thoreau is always aware of
the limits of science; and in his last years he seems especially aware of
the possibility that the decay of the modern world will leave the
schooled eye with nothing worth observing. But he also maintains the
belief that training the observer in a recognizably scientific way, and
through recognizably scientific means, is a task of fundamental importance.

So much can be learned from looking at those of his works which
announce themselves as being about the data of natural history—
leaves, fruits, seeds, trees. The role of natural history in his more
elaborate and more wide-ranging works is, not surprisingly, more
complex. The limitations of science, in Thoreau's view, arise not just
because of the threat of extinction or the weakness of any single route
to understanding the full and ultimately mystical richness of nature.
He is certain that there are states of consciousness concerning which
science has no relevance, and to which science contributes little insight. His task, then, would seem to be to teach mankind enough
science so that they could, in the end, move beyond science into that
condition of Transcendental elevation or sainthood which is his great
goal and the particular focus of his greatest work. To the saint, science
is of little use. But Thoreau knows, all too painfully, that this elevated

97

state is not the normal condition of man, not even of Transcendental man, in this fallen world. In the day-to-day fallen state, natural history has very great importance, as a discipline which prepares the mind for blessedness, as a means of finding those mystical facts which may provoke blessedness, and as a vehicle for describing the pursuit of blessedness. This distinction between two radically different states of being tends to produce the apparent paradox of a Thoreau who is an antiscientific scientist.

Sherman Paul summarizes Thoreau's attitude in the late journals as a "steadfast rejection of science."[1] The odd thing about Paul's argument is that it seems to develop toward an exactly opposite conclusion. Having allowed that Thoreau's science was "merely a discipline to the end of greater familiarity"—a qualification, I think, which deserves more than a passing notice—Paul goes on to assert, not a rejection of science, but the *usefulness* of science to Thoreau:

> Instead of signifying his failure, his reliance on science signified a greater maturity and success: to be scientific for Thoreau was not to abandon the ultimate poetic use of the fact, but to be public and objective. He was driven by his studies to know the entire natural environment, and in this great labor, science was an economy . . . His science, his insistence on accuracy, was also an act of social faith; he was a "natural historian" because he used science in the way he did history.[2]

How this squares with a "steadfast rejection of science" is not at all apparent. But it is clear that at the center of the problem lies the issue of method, of finding or devising a way in which the potentially overwhelming "multitude of detail" which comprises "the entire natural environment" can be observed, learned, understood, and used. "Why do precisely these objects which we behold make a world?" is one of Thoreau's central questions in *Walden* (p. 225). It cannot be answered until some certainty is attained about the existence and nature of those objects, and some reliable vantage point is reached from which to behold them. And both preliminary problems can at least be attacked, if not solved, by using the supposedly objective and disciplined methods of science.

Paul, however, insists that Thoreau rejected from the first even the *method* of the naturalist: "This is not to say that the method of the naturalist is a bad method, but rather that for Thoreau it was the wrong method, and that his distrust of it, indeed the guilt he felt in con-

sciously employing it, banished the 'presence' that he hoped to find."[3]
"Distrust" is a fair word for it; but the distrust need not necessarily
lead to repudiation. In "The Natural History of Massachusetts"
Thoreau remarks, "What an admirable training is science for the more
active warfare of life!" (*Excursions,* 106) And, lest we think that he
means science only in "the most comprehensive sense possible," he
goes on to observe how even such a particular and specialized science
as "entomology extends the limits of being in a new direction" (p.
107). There is always in Thoreau a strong element of the notion
(heretical, for a native of Puritan New England) that insight, and
along with it redemption, are earned. To get to know beans requires
hours of hoeing; and the value of "an admirable training" is not
therefore to be dismissed lightly. But science offers as well something
less onerous and demanding: "I would keep some book of natural
history always by me as a sort of elixir" (p. 105).

The significant fact is that the value of science does not, to Thoreau,
depend ultimately upon the accuracy or even the inherent interest of
the scientific source. He acknowledges in his review that the books he
considers "are such as imply more labor than enthusiasm . . . measurements and minute descriptions, not interesting to the general reader"
(*Excursions,* 129–130). Thoreau can "detect several errors . . . and a
more practiced eye would no doubt expand the list" (p. 130). But still
he reads the books, and others like them; and still he finds a value
there. Much has been made of the fact that Thoreau's review very
nearly ignores entirely the volumes which are its supposed subject—a
peculiar way to evaluate even the dullest book. But what the essay
does, again and again, is demonstrate exactly how to *use* volumes of
natural history. The pattern is represented by the following passage:

> It appears from the report that there are about forty quadrupeds
> belonging to the State, and among these one is glad to hear of a few
> bears, wolves, lynxes, and wildcats.
> When our river overflows its banks in the spring, the wind from the
> meadows is laden with a strong scent of musk, and by its freshness
> advertises me of an unexplored wilderness. (*Excursions,* 114)

The paragraph proceeds, rather fitfully, to a consideration of muskrats
and some word-play involving the Musketaquid River. The connection between the list of quadrupeds which Thoreau finds in the report
and the sight of a muskrat swimming across the Concord River is, at

first glance, so tenuous as to be nearly nonexistent; and indeed, even
by Thoreau's standards, "The Natural History of Massachusetts" is
hardly a model of careful and effective transition. But the connection is
there: the reading of natural history leads Thoreau inevitably back to
thinking about his own observations of nature. It is in this way that
facts, even in dull written form, can teach; as later Thoreau finds a
"singular fact" in the "Report on Invertebrate Animals . . . which
teaches [him] to put a new value on time and space" (*Excursions,* 129).
Science, then, teaches us to look ("Nature will bear the closest inspection," p.107), even if late in his life Thoreau's journal records at times
his worry that he is looking too closely, too "microscopically."[4]
Science, however, provides at the same time the opportunity for
transcendence of that realm of fact with which science is normally concerned. The essay is, in part, an assertion of the former value of
science, and a demonstration of the latter.

The Thoreau is, however, unequivocal on one point; while the facts
stored up by natural history may teach, nature itself is the better
teacher: "Nature has taken more care than the fondest parent for the
education and refinement of her children" (*Excursions,* 124). Whatever
the virtues of measurements and minute descriptions, "Nature is
mythical and mystical always" (p. 125). The essay rests on a final
distinction between science (the discipline and method) and true
science, science in its broadest, its etymological and Transcendental
sense, which is a state of consciousness: "The true man of science will
know nature better by his finer organization; he will smell, taste, see,
hear, feel, better than other men"[5] (p. 131).

The same distinction is to be found in the body of the essay.
Thoreau begins by observing that "books of natural history make the
most cheerful winter reading" (*Excursions,* 103). But later he insists
that, even in winter when observation is most trying and uncomfortable, it is better to observe than to read: "In the winter, the botanist
need not confine himself to his books and herbarium, and give over his
outdoor pursuits, but may study a new department of vegetable
physiology, what may be called crystalline botany, then" (p. 126).
Cheerful reading has its limits; and he who is willing (not, we notice,
by abandoning, but rather by extending the name and method of the
scientist) to go beyond "the accession of health" to be found in the
written "reminiscences of luxuriant nature" (p. 103) will find not only
something worth observing at first hand, but in fact something fun-

damental. In crystals, the botanist will discover a new and indeed a more profound science: "Vegetation has been made the type of all growth; but as in crystals the law is more obvious, their material being more simple, and for the most part more transient and fleeting, would it not be as philosophical as convenient to consider all growth, all filling up within the limits of nature, but a crystallization more or less rapid?" (p. 128).

That the distinction between natural history and nature itself, between the sciences and true science, is fundamental to Thoreau is of course not in question. But that this distinction rests on the assumption that the more ordinary sciences are in any way to be rejected as invalid or wrong, seems to be a considerable overstatement of the case. It is this early essay, we remember, that closes by praising even the pioneer who raises no flowers. As he grew older, Thoreau seems to have found increasingly frequent occasion on which to wonder if perhaps he himself could do no more than sow the seeds of another man's crop; and thus it is not surprising that he seemed at times restless and unsatisfied to be no *more* than a natural historian. But he never completely lost the conviction that science provided at least a vehicle of approach to the "mystical and mythical." Indeed at times he seems to have found in the very materials of science an almost magical transforming power. Here, late in his life, he considers the value of scientific names:

> How hard one must work in order to acquire his language, — words by which to express himself! I have known a particular rush, for instance, for at least twenty years, but have ever been prevented from describing some of its peculiarities, because I did not know its name nor anyone in the neighborhood who could tell me it. With the knowledge of the name comes a distincter recognition and knowledge of the thing. That shore is now more describable, and poetic even. My knowledge was cramped and confined before, and grew rusty because not used, — for it could not be used. My knowledge now becomes communicable and grows by communication. I can now learn what others know about the same thing. (*Journal*, XI, 137; 29 Aug. 1858)

Even allowing for its roots in Part IV of Emerson's *Nature,* the emotional force of the passage seems in excess of its explicit meaning. Precisely how the learning of the name of the plant enlarges Thoreau's ability to describe its peculiarities is not at first clear. But the tremendous importance placed on the finding of names, which at first seems a violation of the kind of calm and objectivity we expect of the scientist, has its roots in naturalism as well as in Transcendentalism. We remember Linnaeus assigning the task of naming as one of the most important obligations of the natural historian; Michel Foucault has argued that this unwavering interest in the correct *words*, the names of things, is a crucial and determining step in the very origins of natural history as a science.[6] What is clear in this case is the importance not only of observing, but of recording and communicating that observation—Thoreau had *known* the plant for years, but now he can describe it and make that description communicable; and it is science that allows the expression.

Perhaps it was his difficulty in establishing a form by which he could fully express, in a generally useful way, the knowledge he spent those last years assembling, that led Thoreau to doubt his accustomed methods. But he had long been aware that there were states of consciousness to which science had no apparent applicability. A long journal entry dating from 1851 attempts to pin down the condition of mind and soul which represents the final leap beyond any mundane science:

July 16. Wednesday. Methinks my present experience is nothing; my past experience is all in all. I think that no experience which I have to-day comes up to or is comparable with, the experiences of my boyhood. And not only this is true, but as far back as I can remember I have unconsciously referred to the experiences of a previous state of existence. "For life is a forgetting," etc. Formerly, methought, nature developed as I developed, and grew up with me. My life was ecstasy. In youth, before I lost any of my senses, I can remember that I was all alive, and inhabited my body with an inexpressible satisfaction; both its weariness and its refreshment were sweet to me. This earth was the most glorious musical instrument, and I was audience to its strains. To have such sweet impressions made on us, such ecstasies begotten of the breezes! I can remember how I was astonished. I said to myself,—I said to others,—"There comes into my mind such an indescribable, infinite, all-absorbing, divine, heavenly pleasure, a sense of elevation and expansion, and I have nought to do with it. I perceive that I am dealt with by superior powers. This is a pleasure, a joy, an existence which I have not procured myself. I speak as a witness on the stand, and tell what I have perceived." The morning and the evening were sweet to me, and I led a life aloof from the society of men. I wondered if a mortal had ever known what I knew. I looked in books for some recognition of a kindred experience, but, strange to say, I found none. Indeed, I was slow to discover that other men had had this experience, for it had been possible to read books and to associate with men on other grounds. The maker of me was improving me. When I detected this interference I was profoundly moved. For years I marched as to a music in comparison with which the military music of the streets is noise and discord. I was daily intoxicated, and yet no man could call me intemperate. With all your science can you tell me how it is, and whence it is, that light comes into the soul? (*Journal*, II, 306–307; 16 July 1851)

Leaving aside for the moment Thoreau's reference to science, the last sentence is a clear restatement, similar in syntax and imagery as in import, of one of the central questions of Romanticism: "Whither is fled the visionary gleam?" It is indeed surprising to find Thoreau claiming that his search in books for "some recognition of a kindred experience" proved unavailing, since he himself acknowledges by misquotation the work which seems most directly to demonstrate "some recognition of a kindred experience," Wordsworth's "Ode: Intimations of Immortality." But in place of the continuous falling away from glory which Wordsworth describes, Thoreau suggests an extended and apparently unchanging, if now lost, state of consciousness: "*For years* I marched," he says, employing a metaphor more familiar in its present-tense version in *Walden*, "as to a music in comparison with which the military music of the streets is noise and discord." The ecstasy is recurrent ("I was *daily* intoxicated"); and it is this elevated state—I will call it Transcendental Sainthood—for which science has no explanation.

Elsewhere Thoreau makes it clear that the state of elevation and expansion is not inevitably lost as one grows older. In an 1841 letter to Isaiah Williams, Thoreau insists on the possibility of "a revelation fresher and director than that" in the New Testament "if any soul look abroad even today" (*Correspondence*, 52; 8 Sept. 1841). In *Walden*, which I take to be Thoreau's most elaborated account of this blessed condition, Thoreau twice recalls youthful visits to the pond; neither case supports the contention that "my present experience is nothing; my past experience is all in all" (*Walden*, 175 and 191). *Walden* as a whole is, to borrow Emerson's term, prospective, full of reawakenings, ranging from that of each morning ("After a partial cessation of his sensuous life, the soul of man, or its organs rather, are reinvigorated each day," (p. 89) to the great reawakening of all Nature in spring ("Walden was dead and is alive again," p. 311). His recasting, from the past to the present tense, of his image of the elevated life as a march is indicative then of the whole course of his thinking.

What is apparent in both the journal and in *Walden* is that to Thoreau there are at least two distinct states of being, the elevated and the fallen, the saintly and quotidian. In the journal entry he locates these two states in time, in the past and the present; in *Walden* he acknowledges that time is not the appropriate framework for such a distinction. In both cases, however, the question that concerns him is, "how it is, and whence it is, that light comes into the soul." More than that, *Walden* takes up the problem of finding adequate expression for the saintly condition. "Heaven speaks, but what language does it use to preach to men?" he had asked, paraphrasing Confucius in 1843 (*Dial,* III, 494; April 1843). His answer then was silence and action; but neither will serve a writer. In *Walden,* as we will see, one of Thoreau's greatest dificulties lies not so much in achieving sainthood, but in preaching from that condition to the fallen state of men around him. The normal means of discourse will not precisely serve, any more than the normal means of accumulating knowledge — science, history — will suffice to explain the nature of sainthood. But Thoreau writes in the everyday world; the condition of sainthood is after all usually silent. As J. L. Shanley has conclusively documented, the account of the holy year was not (as Thoreau repeatedly claimed it was) composed at the time. The journal entry of July 1851 was written in fact very near the time when Thoreau was about to take up his manuscript again, after putting it aside when *A Week* proved such a commercial disappointment.[7] What the experience of writing and rewriting *Walden* seems to have proven to Thoreau is that the pastness of the elevated moment is not altogether a reason to lament. The Transcendental event may be most clear and most comprehensible — and thus most communicable, most useful as literary material — after the fact: "Often I can give the truest and most interesting account of any adventure I have had after years have elapsed, for then I am not confused, only the most significant facts surviving in my memory. Indeed, all that continues to interest me after such a lapse of time is sure to be pertinent, and I may safely record all that I remember" (*Journal,* IX, 311; 28 March 1857).

I have perhaps been overindulgent in applying a religious terminology to the "existence which I have not procured myself." But the suggestion for such terminology lies in Thoreau's own language. In the July 1851 journal entry he shies away from identifying specifically the "superior powers" at work and refuses to dignify the "maker of me" with capitalization. In this way he keeps his feet firmly in the natural and earthly, without necessarily involving the supernatural. But the manner in which his ecstasy is described is both implicitly and explicitly religious. "The morning and the evening were sweet to me" carries a weight of allusive reference to Genesis and to Revelation; and "an indescribable, infinite, all-absorbing, divine, heavenly pleasure" granted by "superior powers" is a state perilously close to an old-style conversion experience.

But if it is religious, the moment lacks a recognizable God. Even if Thoreau's brand of blessedness may at times seem to him to be unprocured, it is usually a clear result of activity and, as Emerson would have it, of self-reliance. Thoreau says (speaking particularly of chastity, "the flowering of man" of which "Holiness, and the like, are but various fruits") that "Nature is hard to be overcome, but she must be overcome" (*Walden*, 219–221). And he could hardly be accused of having that strong and consistent sense of personal inadequacy which is inherent in more traditional (and especially Protestant) descriptions of the Pentecostal moment. In his repeated lists of cardinal virtues in *Walden* he never overlooks simplicity (which is to him an active and deliberate, not a passive and accidental virtue) and never mentions humility.[8] More orthodox writers would agree with him that "the maker of me was improving me" only if they chose to ignore Thoreau's equation of subject and object.

To assert, in any case, that there are transcendent states of consciousness does not resolve the problems of understanding and expressing those states. The July 1851 journal entry, not unexpectedly, will not answer its own questions. If the experience was "improving," why does it leave behind such a sense of present loss? Where, and why, in other words, did the progress stop and the decline begin? Does his youthful sense that "nature developed as I developed, and grew up with me" represent a profound sense of communion, now lost, or a childish solipsism? In *Walden*, being all alive, inhabiting the body with inexpressible satisfaction, takes on a coloring of animality and brutishness—it is closer to the ecstasy of Alek Therien than to Thoreau's. The entry turns, in a way, on the phrase which refers to losing one's senses. Strictly construed, the loss is a bad thing; the true man of science does not lose his senses, and the colloquial meaning of the phrase connects it with simple madness, a loss, rather than a gain, in understanding. But in *Walden* Thoreau considers the profit to be gained by "being beside ourselves in a sane sense," by being "completely lost" as a way of, indeed as a necessary first step toward, appreciating the "vastness and strangeness of Nature" (*Walden*, 135, 171). That is not quite the same as losing one's senses, but it tends that way, and suggests that Thoreau would have us continue to hope for (and not only to lament the loss of) "that light [which] comes into the soul."

IT IS in relation to this state of elevation and expansion that Thoreau expresses his doubts about the value of science, specifically about the ability of science to offer an explanation of ecstasy. What keeps Thoreau from generalizing this skepticism to a wholesale rejection of "your science" is the awareness that the blessed condition, in which revelation, rather than investigation or explanation, is the operative and informing force, is at best occasional and customarily short-lived, and that it touches only the small number of the Elect. In those periods—July 1851 was apparently one of them—when the light fails, one can at least fall back on the more mundane pursuits of knowledge which, after all, do still constitute "an admirable training . . . for the more active warfare of life." Thoreau frames his assertion of his own holiness with a certain Yankee irony, and he too has his times of self-doubt, although usually in a curiously generalized way: "We are conscious of the animal within us, which awakens in proportion as our higher nature slumbers. It is reptile and sensual, and perhaps cannot be wholly expelled; like the worms which, even in life and health, occupy our bodies. Possibly we may withdraw from it, but never change its nature. I fear that it may enjoy a certain health of its own; that we may be well, yet not pure" (*Walden*, 219). Thoreau set himself, as Perry Miller put it, the task of discovering "how to be conscious of the self in a commonplace, prosperous American town"—which I take to be the Transcendental equivalent of living a holy life in a fallen world.[9] Miller cannot, in the end, forgive Thoreau his apparent arrogance: "[He] fought . . . to be a partner with the Almighty. Obviously he who strives to play the drama of such arrogance on the solid soil of Massachusetts is heading as recklessly as Tamburlaine or Faust toward catastrophe."[10] One wonders where, precisely, to seek the catastrophe; surely not in "Wild Apples" or the other late essays. Miller misses the degree to which the arrogance was turned against the self; the contemptuous tone of "with all your science" is surely directed as much toward Thoreau himself as toward the world. In any case, the effort toward sainthood, of his own sort, was for Thoreau "a distinct profession," even, as Sherman Paul argues, a vocation.[11]

It was this admittedly and intentionally eccentric sense of profession which contributed as well to Thoreau's refusal to accept at common value the name of scientist or historian. Asked to describe himself for a tenth-year report of his Harvard class, Thoreau insisted on the inadequacy of those professional labels which a more worldly soul might have accepted willingly:

> I don't know whether mine is a profession, or a trade, or what not. It is not yet learned, and in every instance has been practiced before being studied. The mercantile part of it was begun here by myself alone.
> —It is not one but legion. I will give you some of the monster's heads. I am a schoolmaster—a Private Tutor, a Surveyor—a Gardener, a Farmer—a Painter, I mean a House Painter, a Carpenter, a Mason, a Day-laborer, a Pencil-Maker, a Glass-paper Maker, a Writer, and sometimes a Poetaster. (*Correspondence*, 186; 30 Sept. 1847)[12]

As at the top of Ktaadn, Thoreau chooses to identify himself with the evil spirits, in this case the demon whose name is Legion (Mark V:1–13). Thoreau declines the honor, not only of a profession, but even of the use of the *word* profession. But we should not let the harsh manner of the letter obscure the fact that he might, on the basis of skill or remunerative employment or, indeed, careful study, have accepted most if not all of the names he lists. His refusal of labels—even, most surprisingly, of the title writer or poet—represents less a turning away from these "trades or what not" than a clear assertion that he is all these, and more if he wishes.

So too with the name of scientist or historian or natural historian$if he adopts none of them as wholly and all-inclusively his own, still he practices the methods and professions they encompass seriously, in his own way. Hawthorne, who insisted that "Mr. Thorow is a keen and delicate observer of nature—a genuine observer, which, I suspect, is almost as rare a character as even an original poet," also recognized that his then young friend would live "in a way and method of his own."[13] That way would be inclusive, not exclusive; and even "in Arcadia when I was there" (*Walden*, 57), even on the shores of mystic

Walden, dead and born again like Christ in the Creed, he could find a way to employ science, if not as a source of explanations, then at least as a mode of inquiry. As a man who knows carpentry and hoeing, Thoreau knows too the proper use of any tool, as of any method—what it will do and what it will not do: "No method nor discipline can supersede the necessity of being forever on the alert. What is a course of history, or philosophy, or poetry, no matter how well selected, or the best of society, or the most admirable routine of life, compared with the discipline of looking always at what is to be seen? Will you be a reader, a student merely, or a seer? Read your fate, see what is before you, and walk into futurity" (p. 111).[14] One of the many peculiarities of *Walden* is that it is a book which carries within it the hope that one day, if it is read properly, it will not need to be read at all.

THOREAU'S attitude toward science, then, is not so much a repudiation as it is a constant wariness. Robert Langbaum has remarked that "The Romanticist is not against science. He is merely trying to limit the applicability of its findings."[15] In this regard, as in others, Thoreau is clearly Romantic. In *Walden* he is concerned with the blessed condition and the blessed place—a condition and a place in which the applicability of science is especially limited. The question he had raised in his journal in July 1851 is thus peculiarly relevant: "With all your science can you tell me how it is, and whence it is, that light comes into the soul?" Remarkably enough, the science of natural history is to be found, and even used, in Eden, as a closer look at *Walden* may help to demonstrate.

Thoreau's most direct answer in *Walden* to the "very particular inquiries . . . made by my townsmen concerning my mode of life" (p. 3) is this: "I went to the woods because I wished to live deliberately, to front only the essential facts of life, and to see if I could not learn what it had to teach" (p. 90). This combines two tasks in one formula: observation (fronting the facts) and discrimination (fronting only the essential). The nature of living deliberately thus calls directly for the habits of the naturalist, and of course in addition the frame of mind of the mystic. And, since Thoreau sets himself the added task of speaking precisely to and about the condition of "you who read these pages, who are said to live in New England" (p. 4), he must be an evangelist, the effect of whose speech would, in the ideal, be utterly transforming: "There are probably words addressed to our condition exactly, which, if we could really hear and understand, would be more salutary than the morning or the spring to our lives, and possibly put a new aspect on the face of things for us" (p. 107).

This peculiar combination of roles—naturalist, mystic, evangelist—is not an easy one; as mystic, Thoreau distrusts the very methods he must employ as a naturalist. As a preacher, he finds the record of observed phenomena to be, at the least, a useful vehicle of communication; but he also knows that many of the things of which he must speak are incommunicable. He ends up, paradoxically, writing a natural history of Eden, or at least a natural history of bliss.

Repeatedly he insists on the *possibility* of blessedness—"man's capacities have never been measured; nor are we to judge of what he can do by any precedents, so little has been tried" (*Walden,* 10). So much then for authority and received wisdom—"What old people say you cannot do you try and find that you can. Old deeds for old people, and new deeds for new" (p. 8). But it is not, unfortunately, enough to assert the necessity for a new way of life, nor to repeat the virtues of the new dispensation, "simplicity, independence, magnanimity, and trust" (p. 15). Even though the place and the state of salvation are, at bottom, simple, symmetrical, *not* detailed ("Our life is frittered away by detail," p. 91), salvation can, in the present world, only be pursued and described by means of detail—names, measurements, accounts, arithmetic. And as we will see, it is inherent in the kind of resolutely *individual* revelation which Thoreau finds that it cannot be passed on. The most he can hope to offer his readers is the inspiration and reassurance which they may draw from being shown that the goal is attainable and has indeed been attained. At the same time he produces a cautionary record of how difficult the path will be.

Walden is a book, then, that not only contradicts but criticizes itself.[16] Much is made, as I have said, of Thoreau's arrogance, of the Transcendental egotism which allows him to write a saint's life of himself. His apology—"I should not talk so much about myself if there were any body else whom I knew as well" (*Walden,* 3)—is too disingenuous and rather too quickly gotten over to answer the charge satisfactorily. We are dealing with a peculiar kind of sainthood, one which includes among its aspects irony and anger and excludes the note of humility we find more usual and more to our taste. But it is a sainthood which does not insist, indeed does not expect or desire, emulation in any exact way; the arrogance of this saint's manner is in part a prophylaxis against the too easy path of simple imitation. Part of the science of this self-hagiographer is to establish for us the distance we need to observe saintliness safely and productively; there is, as Thoreau remarks in passing while considering the pickerel of Walden, great danger in being translated before our time "to the thin air of heaven" (p. 285).

I use the word saint with no more apology; I read *Walden* as, in part at least, an autobiographical saint's life. We must not take as absolutely true either the assertions we find in it (since many of the most direct and forthright statements in the book are explicitly contradicted elsewhere between its covers) or the often jocular self-deprecation which surrounds some of its most important moments. And we must never lose the paradoxical yardstick of approximation, no matter how many apparently hard, well-documented facts and numbers we find in it. The nature of this kind of sainthood is that it is achievable and definite, if rare, but not quite earnable. It is thus at once deliberate and accidental, procured and providential. And, if it is recurrent (like the rise and fall of Walden Pond, like the movement of seasons from Spring to Spring), it is also, in its recognizable form, passing and largely inexpressible except in the inadequate language of the fallen state. Indeed, the fundamental questions that continually drive Thoreau toward the Pentecostal insight he finds at Walden are a sign of his own fallen nature, his own unnaturalness:

> After a still winter night I awoke with the impression that some questions had been put to me, which I had been endeavoring in vain to answer in my sleep, as what—how—when—where? But there was dawning Nature, in whom all creatures live, looking in at my broad windows with serene and satisfied face, and no question on *her* lips. I awoke to an unanswered question, to Nature and daylight. The snow lying deep on the earth dotted with young pines, and the very slope of the hill on which my house is placed, seemed to say, Forward! Nature puts no question and answers none which we mortals ask. (*Walden,* 282)

The questions about which science has nothing to say (how it is, where it is, whence it is that light comes into the soul) are the questions which trouble this saint. The written answers to such questions will, looked at one way, be yet another second-hand account, an "authority" of sorts, useful only in "homeopathic doses" (p. 167), but useful nevertheless, if used warily. Having early on insisted that experience is invariably preferable to advice (p. 9), and having, as a beginning farmer, refused to be "in the least awed by many celebrated works on husbandry" (p. 55), Thoreau still loses few chances to study, "consulting such authorities as offered" even when he sets out to make bread (p. 62).

THE PRECISE connection between human knowledge and revelation, between science and sainthood, is played out in the sequence of chapters from "The Village" to "Baker Farm." The trip begins among the most fallen and moves to and just beyond one of the principal Pentecostal moments in *Walden,* Thoreau's attainment of his halo; at the same time Thoreau proceeds from naturalizing of various sorts to inspiration to attempted evangelism, when he tries to convert the Irishman John Field. The chapters are, in many ways, central in the book; most obviously, the chapter on "The Ponds," the middle of the three we will be considering, is the ninth of the seventeen chapters of *Walden.*

"The Village" follows Thoreau's extended discussion of how he earned his living, in the reformed sense, by hoeing beans, and tells how he spent the resulting "absolutely free" time (*Walden,* 167). We remember how much of *Walden* is intended to show us that we *waste* time getting and spending. "The Bean-Field" (and, of course, "Economy") demonstrates how little time we really need to fulfill our economic needs. That means we will have more time to spend elsewhere. It is at first surprising to discover that "every day or two [Thoreau] strolled to the village to hear some of the gossip which is incessantly going on there, circulating either from mouth to mouth, or from newspaper to newspaper" (p. 167). Earlier Thoreau had insisted, "I am sure that I never read any memorable news in a newspaper" (p. 94), and "Economy" makes it clear how little sympathy he has for that village in which man "has no time to be anything but a machine" (p. 6), and toward whose expectations he is deliberately antipathetic: "The greater part of what my neighbors call good I believe in my soul to be bad, and if I repent of anything, it is very likely to be my good behavior. What demon possessed me that I behaved so well?" (p. 10). But if we have been paying attention, we also know that Thoreau "love[s] society as much as most." "I am naturally no hermit, but might possibly sit out the sturdiest frequenter of the bar-room, if my business called me thither" (p. 140).

Still, a visit to the village is a visit, as it soon becomes apparent, to a fallen and dead world, the locus and visible sign of the deadening way of life detailed in "Economy." Thoreau goes to Concord as a naturalist: "As I walked in the woods to see the birds and squirrels, so I walked in the village to see the men and boys; instead of the wind among the pines I heard the carts rattle. In one direction from my house there was a colony of muskrats in the river meadows; under the grove of elms and buttonwoods in the other horizon was a village of busy men, as curious to me as if they had been prairie dogs, each sitting at the mouth of its burrow, or running over to a neighbor's to gossip" (*Walden*, 167). How seriously Thoreau intends the polarity suggested here by his talk of two horizons will be made clearer at the beginning of "Baker Farm" when he again walks to a grove of trees, and finds among its flora "the *Celtis occidentalis*, or false elm" (p. 202).[17] That grove, however, contains a shrine, not a village. In the present case, if we know Thoreau's favorite beasts, the polarity is the opposite of what a naive reader might think; the muskrat is an especially well-regarded animal to this naturalist, and village man is not. These brute neighbors might better be prairie dogs. As at John Field's house, where the only order of being explicitly identified as human is the chicken, not the Irish (p. 204), "animal nature" here in Concord is considerably more lively than man. The town has "digestive organs"—but only for news, which, of course, in this Nowhere is no news. The row of worthies Thoreau observes, despite their occasionally "voluptuous" expressions, are no more than stone caryatids (p. 168). The village moves but does not live; its "vitals" are stores, not heart and belly, and the most elaborately described activity— the "gantlet" which Thoreau escapes only "wonderfully" (pp. 168–169)—is, on close inspection, an activity not of men but of houses. The chapter, as it quickly turns out, is, despite its relatively warm and good-humored beginning, not about the village but about escaping from it.[18] The observer, by detailing the landscape of hell, learns how to avoid it. Having investigated the world of "machines" (p. 168), of lines, lanes, traps, and bizarre but clear-cut orderings, a world where the primary sense to be employed by the naturalist is the eye, Thoreau launches himself (the nautical image is his own) into the woods, where the only way to find one's route is to feel with feet and hands (p. 169) and where the "most surprising and memorable, as well as valuable experience" is to be invisible and lost. That experience is available, however, only to the enlightened; the villagers become lost frequently, without apparent gain (p. 170). The moral is clear and clearly pointed: "not till we have lost the world, do we begin to find ourselves" (p. 171). It is the version, in this Transcendental scripture, of the parable of the rich man and the eye of the needle (Matthew XIX: 16–30). The chapter ends, however, not with this text but rather with a very brief account of Thoreau's seizure for taxes — another warning sign of the dangerously entrapping force of the village and of men's "dirty institutions." The only safeguard (like the only means of escape from the gantlet, which was by "keeping my thoughts on higher things" (p. 169)), is to be found in "the virtues of the superior man" (p. 172).

The effect, then, of naturalizing hell is to warn; but what of naturalizing heaven? "The Ponds" is Thoreau's most extended description of Walden itself. He gets there — and away from "human society and gossip" — by proceeding in the mystical direction, westward, and by renewing his direct experience of nature, plucking and tasting blueberries on Fair Haven Hill (*Walden*, 173). Thoreau likes to begin his natural histories with instructive parables rather than facts.[19] Here he tells us of the Cenobitic fisherman, a kind of society less dangerous than the town of Concord; and then he recounts his youthful misunderstanding of Walden, at a time when he could still happily return from its banks to the "haunts of men."

Finally he describes in some detail an instance of escape (*Walden*, 173–175). Again the experience is "memorable and valuable." He leaves a "village parlor" and fishes by night, "partly with a view to the next day's dinner" but, more important, to restore his senses. The fable contains one of the better known moments in *Walden:* that time when, letting his thoughts "wander to vast and cosmogonal themes in other spheres," he has the great luck to "catch two fishes as it were with one hook." A real fish tugs at his line, destined for that next day's supper; a metaphysical one appears in the same moment, a sign of the productive loss of orientation and of the re-establishment of the link to Nature (pp. 174–175).

It is a reminder to us that the true scientist wants both fact and symbol and seeks those best moments when the two spheres meet. Having established a safe context, Thoreau now adopts the full-blown manner of the naturalist: "The scenery of Walden is on a humble scale, and though very beautiful, does not approach grandeur, nor can it much concern one who has not long frequented it or lived by its shore; yet this pond is so remarkable for its depth and purity as to merit a particular description" (*Walden,* 175).[20] The chapter proceeds to prove, and to disprove, this statement, and establishes, in hard detail, both the uniqueness and the symbolic typicality of the place. Nothing could be more matter-of-fact than Thoreau's initial description of the pond: "It is a clear and deep green well, half a mile long and a mile and three quarters in circumference, and contains about sixty-one and a half acres; a perennial spring in the midst of pine and oak woods, without any visible inlet or outlet except by the clouds and evaporation" (p. 175). But because this is Thoreau and not Gilbert White, one immediately begins to subject these facts to a pressure of interpretation. Clarity and depth point directly to the question of finding bottom in "The Pond in Winter" (pp. 282–298). The precision of the measurements here forewarn us about the astounding (and, to the layman's eye, unlikely) symmetry of the pond's shape (p. 289).[21] The question of inlet and outlet is raised again (p. 292) and related to a world-wide transmigration of waters (pp. 297–298); that the only apparent outlet is the sky raises the point that part of Walden's uniqueness is the way in which it *combines* elements into Sky Water (pp. 188–189). Most striking of all is the phrase "perennial spring," for it is the peculiar timelessness of Walden and its recurrent awakening in spring ("Walden was dead and is alive again") that lie at the heart of its symbolic value. The passage is, as promised, a particular description — color, size, shape, volume — as well as an introduction to a whole series of symbolic developments to come. Thoreau proceeds, in the short run, to develop each of the points raised, in proper sequence: color (pp. 176–177); transparency and purity (pp. 177–178); circumference (pp. 178–179); rise and fall, by whatever inlet or outlet (pp. 180–182).

Each step in the fully elaborated description is a repetition of the synthesis of detail and metaphor to be found in the introductory sentences. The question of color, for example, is related directly to known and observable phenomena — effects of light, weather, and distance. But quickly the larger point is established: in science as well as in symbol, the pond is intermediary, since, "lying between the earth and the heavens, it partakes of the color of both." And the pond, even in winter, is the "vivid green" of rejuvenation; so, later, the arrival of spring occurs in a chapter entitled "The Pond in *Winter*." And color, intimately related to vision, allows Thoreau, while describing the precise scientific reasons for Walden's thawing near the shore, to make the pond an Emersonian eyeball: "Such is the color of its iris." The development of that point he saves until a few pages later (p. 186). At the moment, the observation of the pond allows Thoreau to look "with divided vision," and thus to see twice at once, as he had just before in catching his two fish at once and as he will later be able, in puddles, to be beside himself in a sane sense by seeing himself stand on his head (p. 293). Finally, color involves purity, and the purity of this water is part of its ritual, baptismal effect. "The body of a bather" in Walden, unlike that of a bather elsewhere, "appears of an alabaster whiteness." The suggestion of baptism is both a clue and a puzzle; this baptism is, initially at least, "unnatural"—but it is also fruitful in art, "making fit studies for a Michel Angelo."

The color of Walden, then, as it is described by Thoreau, can serve as an exemplification of the way in which the macrocosm of the book is almost entirely contained within the microcosm of a paragraph, and of the way Thoreau proceeds *both* naturalistically and Transcendentally —and, in each case, to much the same point. The accumulation of facts establishes the general case of Walden's uniqueness, and the specific nature of that uniqueness—a task of definition and description, of natural history. But, at the same time, any individual fact, fronted deliberately and imaginatively, generates symbolic understanding. Thoreau insists that it is the *single* fact which will redeem: "When one man has reduced a fact of the imagination to be a fact to his understanding, I foresee that all men will at length establish their lives on that basis" (*Walden,* 11). And a single fact will be the test of our redemption: "If we knew all the laws of Nature, we should need only one fact, or the description of one actual phenomenon, to infer all the particular results at that point" (p. 280). Looked at either way—indeed looked at many ways at once, literally, scientifically, imaginatively, symbolically—the facts lead inexorably to the conclusion that Walden is unique and uniquely instructive,[22] both a mediator ("intermediate . . . between land and sky," p. 199) and a standard of measurement ("how much more beautiful than our lives, how much more transparent than our characters," p. 199).

We have had in these two chapters natural history as warning, as a means of insight, and as a source of symbol. Having immersed himself in ponds (as he does, more literally, before daring to venture against the dangers of the village), Thoreau is ready to wander where the transforming spirit might find or follow him. That wandering takes him eventually to Baker Farm, home of, among others, John Field, his brave but slovenly wife, starveling sibylline brats, and chickens. But first he encounters a series of magic places, grove-temples, worthy of Druids and Norse gods (*Walden,* 201). "Baker Farm" begins with a compendium of mysteries — temples built by no human hand, fleets on dry land, Valhalla, and swamp gods, all appearing in one (admittedly long) sentence. At the same time the places are intensely real and detailed. The catalogue includes twenty different plants, each correctly and specifically named (pp. 201–202). As fits such a complex and, initially, puzzling place, it is disturbing and even ominous: "The wild-holly berries make the beholder forget his home with their beauty, and he is dazzled and tempted by nameless other wild forbidden fruits, too fair for mortal taste" (p. 201). That leaves moot the question of whether this is Eden or Lotus-Land; and it makes this place (which is, in good mystical form, many places) a suitable counterweight for the ambiguities of the village, which is also, in its own way, both alluring and dangerous. Unexpectedly, the Pentecostal moment occurs:

> Once it chanced that I stood in the very abutment of a rainbow's arch, which filled the lower stratum of the atmosphere, tinging the grass and leaves around, and dazzling me as if I looked through colored crystal. It was a lake of rainbow light, in which, for a short while, I dived like a dolphin. If it had lasted longer it might have tinged my employments and life. As I walked on the railroad causeway, I used to wonder at the halo of light around my shadow, and would fain fancy myself one of the elect. One who visited me declared that the shadows of some Irishmen before him had no halo about them, that it was only the natives that were so distinguished. Benvenuto Cellini tells us in his memoirs, that, after a certain terrible dream or vision, which he had during his confinement in the castle of St. Angelo, a resplendent light appeared over the shadow of his head at morning and evening, whether he was in Italy or France, and it was particularly conspicuous when the grass was moist with dew. This was probably the same phenomenon to which I have referred, which is especially observed in the morning, but also at other times, and even by moonlight. Though a constant one, it is not commonly noticed, and, in the case of an excitable imagination like Cellini's, it would be basis enough for superstition. Beside, he tells us that he showed it to very few. But are they not indeed distinguished who are conscious that they are regarded at all? (pp. 202–203)

Thoreau has prepared himself—and us—for this visitation by going carefully over the ground of heaven and hell in the previous chapters. And we must not be misled by the self-deprecation here; this is indeed a visitation, and no mistake. In fact it is two visitations, one accidental, single, and improbable, the second constant and more commonly available. The first—Thoreau's moment at the end of the rainbow—apparently occurs in or near one of the shrines which he has just told us he "visited both summer and winter." It transforms both Thoreau and the whole "lower" world; it distorts his vision, which, as elsewhere, seems to be paradoxically a good thing. And of course, the visible sign is "a *lake* of rainbow light." That he dives like a dolphin suggests both the legend of Arion the poet (and, by extension, of Thoreau the poet) and, perhaps, the Pauline description of God: "In Him we live, and move, and have our being" (Acts XVII:28). By becoming a dolphin Thoreau succeeds in gaining the clearest sign of redemption offered in *Walden:* the confusion of elements. He has already tended this way by seeing the air as crystal; now he continues by identifying himself as an air-breathing water-beast, the only possible being able to survive in a lake of light, or in a pond which is sky-water.

Rather abruptly, it seems, the moment passes. Thoreau moves on to another experience—a sign of the first having occurred, a kind of stigmatical aura?—the halo around his shadow. The associative links are clear enough, primarily light and Election, but the experiences are not necessarily related, even as phenomena of science. But if we recall Gilbert White's account of the shower of cobwebs or the leper of Selborne, we can at least recognize the familiar pattern of investigation. Thoreau begins with a striking, indeed unique ("*Once it chanced* . . ."(experience. He then looks abroad for any sort of analogous phenomenon, particularly a recurrent one (thus providing more evidence) and reviews his own experience (which is less susceptible to the distortion of report). The closest parallel to be found—and the initial event is so unusual that neither we nor he should expect a close match—occurs on the railroad causeway. In that way the Pentecostal moment is returned to the literal shores of Walden Pond, and to the very place which, although it is the lair of the "devilish Iron Horse" (*Walden,* 192), is to be the scene of the great final resurrection in "Spring" (pp. 304–309). The natural historian, keeping his mystical side alive by linking the phenomenon, ironically, to Election, finds in the more customary phenomenon the material of reasoned investigation. The sources of information are the expected ones: personal observation, second-hand contemporary report (from "one who visited me"), and historical document.[23] The lesson to be drawn by the naturalist is that the problem is one of observation, not of occurrence; that is, if those who had eyes to see *did* see, the constancy of such visitations would no longer be missed. There is no absence of such moments in the fallen world, but only a failure of fallen consciousness, which sets off the generality of men even from the superstitious souls who misinterpret the halo, but who nevertheless at least know the regard (that is, esteem) which any man could feel.

The passage, which has tried in the manner of the naturalist to separate sense from superstition, ends with a resolution that is also a verbal puzzle. Who is it who *regards* the distinguished few? If the word is taken to mean *observe,* then the observer is either the self (if the distinction is a personal recognition of election) or, perhaps, the world at large. The common run of men regard the saved as at least different, even if they can only see this as eccentricity; so Thoreau played the role of the town eccentric, or worse. That sort of regard is what lead to the writing of *Walden:* "I would not obtrude my affairs so much on the notice of my readers if very particular inquiries had not been made by my townsmen concerning my mode of life, which some would call impertinent" (*Walden,* 3). The sign of redemption seems, then, to be a combination of self-awareness and the wary, indeed often hostile observation of the saint by the lost.[24]

The style of the natural historian provides a vehicle whereby the complexities of the moment can be organized and expressed. Thoreau's description and the lesson he draws from it are, in intention, the least naturalistic points imaginable. The passage combines in a very short space many of the important elements of the book as a whole: sainthood, the railroad, the confusion of elements, the symbolism of limnology, the theme of the productive imprecision of the elevated senses. The visitor who offers Thoreau some information (apparently wrong, since Cellini is no native), raises at the same time the troublesome issue of the Irish (which will crop up again barely a page later when John Field appears) and the question of who is more saved or more redeemable, strangers or natives. The mention of Cellini's finding and recording the same phenomenon far distant in space and time, at first seems to undercut the identification of Walden as the holy place. But in fact the idea that such a visitation can occur even in France (a most fallen land, to judge from Thoreau's hostility to the French in *A Yankee in Canada*) emphasizes again that sainthood is a state of consciousness, and that Walden is a holy place only in the symbolic realm, not necessarily in the physical. Thoreau put the matter squarely in a letter to Isaiah Williams: "It is curious that while you are sighing for New England the scene of our fairest dreams should lie in the west — it confirms in me the opinion that places are well nigh indifferent. Perhaps you have experienced that in proportion as our love of Nature is deep and pure we are independent upon her" (*Correspondence*, 53; 8 Sept. 1841).[25] It is fitting that, wherever they occur, these moments are "especially observed in the morning," the time, throughout *Walden*, of awakening in both the physical and the spiritual sense (*Walden*, 282). Thoreau's problem as a writer is how to control so much complexity of reference, how to render an account of something that is, in its way, unaccountable; and the methods of the natural historian are readily at hand.

The problem of how to express the nature and accessibility, to the "conscious" being, of the redeemed condition, is the issue of the remainder of the chapter. Thoreau continues by recounting the story of one particular walk, to the meadow near Baker Farm. He remembers the days before he himself was in the least redeemed — "I thought of living there before I went to Walden. I 'hooked' the apples, leaped the brook, and scared the musquash and the trout" (*Walden*, 203). The day proves unpropitious for fishing, and Thoreau finds shelter in a hut "fabled" to be by "a poet builded" (pp. 203–204), but now the home of "John Field, Irishman." Field is an ideal subject for evangelism, if Thoreau is right about the "constancy" of sainthood, its availability to any man whose consciousness is altered. Field is a stranger, but he has clearly "settled," and one assumes he has lived near Walden about as long as Thoreau has actually been in residence. Field works hard, but altogether wrongly; just as the society scrutinized in "Economy" does. Thoreau is moved to preach — "I tried to help him with my experience" (p. 205) — and proceeds, in a long sentence, to summarize much of the matter of *Walden*. The sermon ends with the expected points: that redemption is not a place and that the real task is not hoeing but *self*-culture. The message fails to take hold: John Field and his wife will go on living "bravely, after their fashion, face to face," but still lost (p. 206).

That the sermon fails is not surprising; moreover, since its matter is so close to that of *Walden,* it is an omen of the possibility that *Walden* itself will fall on equally deaf ears. But after all, Thoreau knows that experience cannot be passed on — that the past, however recent, cannot be straightforwardly presented. What that means, to a writer who wishes to render a useful account of his own exemplary life, is problematical. At the very least, the product will not be a guidebook. In the immediate instance, Thoreau sets off after another rainbow (*Walden,* 206) and falls into some despair. He tries to look down the well, since bottom is always restorative to him, but cannot see it; instead he drinks water that is as unlike the pure fluid of Walden as one could imagine (p. 206). He wanders in the wilderness; and not the restorative wilderness, but that of ordeal, of the forty-days' test, full of "sloughs and bog holes . . . forlorn and savage places" (p. 207). But the despair is not final; Thoreau finds, or rather gives himself ("my good Genius seemed to say . . .") a prophecy. The language is unmistakably biblical, and the message is unmistakably individualistic: cultivate yourself. The prophecy is, like the sermon to Field, a summary in small of *Walden;* but now, not of the facts but of their meaning (pp. 207–208). The chapter ends with some hope even for the fallen John Field. He is moved to find Thoreau again, now "with an altered mind." The two men fish, and of course John catches nothing. Thoreau laments the Irishman's fate: "Poor John Field! — I trust he does not read this, unless he will improve by it, — thinking to live by some derivative old country mode in this primitive new country, — to catch perch with shiners" (p. 208). All hope is not lost — "It is good bait sometimes, I allow." Field, poor man that he is, but poor at least in the right way (pp. 34–35 and 196), is specifically identified with the first of the fallen, Adam, and so damned ("not to rise in this world, he nor his posterity") — but only, perhaps, provisionally ("till their wading webbed bog-trotting feet get *talaria* to their heels"). Thoreau will not in any case stop preaching; he proceeds, without more hesitation than a change of chapters, to make of his walk home from the fishing expedition a sermon on "Higher Laws."

ALTHOUGH science may not be able to tell us "how it is, and whence it is, that light comes into the soul," natural history has its use, even to the elect and even in Eden, as the source of instructive and admonitory information about the fallen, a way of uncovering facts to be studied

Transcendentally, a means of description of the holy places, and a method of organization. Natural history is a way of speaking to the fallen, of providing the closest available approximation of the Celestial City to those not yet ready for its thin air. So, in "The Pond in Winter," Thoreau spends a great deal of time measuring Walden by the world's standards, and in the process emphasizes the more significant symbolic truth of the necessity of settling down to the bottom, while pointing out as well the usual limitations of man's vision and the final import of Walden's symmetry. The effect is natural history as parable, the physical act of measuring serving to exemplify the imaginative and spiritual act of fronting the essential facts, of overseeing all the details ourselves in person (*Walden*, 20). The science involved is not a source of insight so much as it is a vehicle for the representation of insight; the commonness of the reported experience (the plumbing, by the most obvious of means, of a humble pond which cannot much concern one who has not long frequented it) is a sign of the proximity of grace, which, though constant, is not commonly noticed. So, too, the recognizability of the methods—common sense and observation—allows to the fallen at least the possibility of comprehension. The result of the descent of the tongues of fire upon the heads of the Apostles at Pentecost was to let them speak in all the tongues of men; the listening multitude "were bewildered, because each one heard them speaking in this own language" (Acts II:6). There may be little hope for John Field or for those of us who are only said to live, but what little there is arises only because Thoreau talks to him and to us in our own tongue of tea, coffee, butter, and milk, of fishing and hoeing, of the most recognizable of "wild" life.

In speaking to the literate, the employment of the mundane (in several senses) and popular methods of the field naturalist serves a similar purpose. But what of history in the more strict sense? It can be argued that *Walden* is in most ways the least historical of Thoreau's longer works. Certainly by comparison to *Cape Cod* or *A Week*, where the written chronicles of New England are explicitly cited again and again, *Walden* is exceedingly sparing in its use of authorities. Such sources are not completely absent; we noticed that Cellini's autobiography was invoked in "Baker Farm." But, as a rough measure, Thoreau mentions in *Walden*, by my count, only four local histories, three of them in "Economy" when he is outlining the debased society he sees around him.[26] Compare this to *Cape Cod*, where the acknowledged authorities include, among others, Beverly's *History of Virginia, Mourt's Relation,* Champlain's *Voyages,* Wood's *New England's Prospect,* Morton's *New England's Canaan,* the *Collections of the Massachusetts Historical Society,* and, at great length, the church records of the town of Eastham.

There is of course history of a kind elsewhere in the book. The vicinity of Thoreau's chosen home near the pond has a past that is largely fable, which constitutes the material of the chapter "Former Inhabitants; and Winter Visitors," in which Thoreau is "obliged to conjure up the former occupants of these woods," slaves, drinkers, and squatters (*Walden,* 256). As conjuration or fable, the past frequently enters into *Walden,* even in the description of the pond itself, which includes, for example, the "Indian fable" of Walden's origin (p. 182). But the question of accuracy does not arise where fable is concerned, as it inevitably does in dealing with history. "The Ponds" offers at least three separate and not especially congruent fables about the origin and age of Walden, one of them purely of Thoreau's own making (p. 179). In the end what concerns him is not the source but the existence of the pond—"It is very certain, at any rate, that once there was no pond here, and now there is one" (p. 182).

Of historical facts of the more commonly valued sort, Walden Pond is blessedly innocent. The former inhabitants are members of that great mass of men of whom history, until very recently, took no notice. Concord's greatest moment of worldly fame, the Concord Fight, occurred only some two miles away, but the Battle Ground, "our only field known to fame," is invisible from Thoreau's seat "by the shore of a small pond" (*Walden,* 86). As for history in the abstract sense, as a field of study or a path to knowledge, Thoreau makes it clear that the redeemed need take no notice of it, for they live at the meeting of two eternities (p. 18) and in that spiritual spring where all histories are irrelevant (p. 310). If for some reason the saint employs history, he does so as a true natural historian would, warily and only as corroboration, always trying and measuring it against the observed present. As Gilbert White had said, "One cannot safely relate any thing from common report . . . without expressing some degree of doubt and suspicion" (*NHS,* 11/28/1768).

History is most often mentioned in Walden in the abstract—"history" rather than "the history of "—and in the negative, as during the sermon to John Field: "For I purposely talked to him as if he were a philosopher, or desired to be one. I should be glad if all the meadows on the earth were left in a wild state, if that were the consequence of men's beginning to redeem themselves. A man will not need to study history to find out what is best for his own culture" (*Walden*, 205). That the dismissal of history follows, on the page, the beginning of redemption is not, I think, merely an accident of syntax. Once saved, indeed, man will not need to study history; the dictum is couched in what we might call the Revelatory Optative. Later, Thoreau dismisses "histories, chronologies, traditions, and all written revelations," but only at the moment of Resurrection, "the year beginning with younger hope than ever!" (p. 310). Alas, as he knows, the mass of men are far from redeemed as yet, the year is not all Spring, and there is still a place for written revelations, even for one called *Walden.* In the meantime, rubbish, especially the accumulation of written accounts, may still be put to use: "By such a pile we may hope to scale heaven at last" (p. 104).

Walden however is a book especially about the elect, rather than the fallen; and as such, it is only right that it should contain little history, and that what history there is should be most prevalent in "Economy," the part of the book in which the false way is being condemned on its own terms. *Cape Cod* by contrast is a journey to and among the fallen; and as we will see it is full of history. But still *Walden* is, in itself, a history—an account of specific events, compiled from first-hand reports and pretending, at least, to be full of the stuff of the most dull and detailed chronicles, a rendering of accounts in the numerical as well as in all other senses. It is in fact, in Emersonian terms, a history of the truest sort; the most accurate history, Thoreau repeatedly insists, that he could write—a history and natural history of the Self.

And, as a natural history should be, *Walden* is a settled, grounded, parochial book. But we remember from our consideration of Darwin that the natural historian can be a traveler as well as a settler. In one sense *Walden* rebuts this idea. Thoreau's assertion that he travels widely in Concord (*Walden*, 4) is a broad clue about the eccentric kind of book he intends. The book is an explicit alternative to books (and to human lives) which presume that discovery and travel are necessarily two words for the same thing. While getting to know beans, Thoreau observes "travellers bound westward"—in his favorite direction—and remarks how he was to them "a very *agricola laboriosus* . . . the home-staying, laborious native of the soil" (p. 157). But that is by no means the conclusion of the book, either in pages or in argument. Indeed, almost the first words of Thoreau's "Conclusion" are, "Thank Heaven, here is not all the world" (p. 320). So much for the absolute virtue of parochialism.

The mistake Thoreau sees travelers making is to confuse activity with method. "Extra-vagance," being beside one's self in a good sense, is not to be confused with physical movement, although, indeed, to Thoreau himself, as to Wordsworth or Whitman or Stevens, true extra-vagance seems most easily to happen while one is walking. Exploration of the proper sort can be done as well or as poorly on the edge of Concord as on the coast of Tierra del Fuego.

We exaggerate, I think, in taking *Walden* too easily as Thoreau's characteristic book—especially that *Walden* which we tend to simplify, in remembrance, as a gospel of Transcendental parochialism. Geographical movement is the apparent organizing principle in the majority of his extended works; *A Week, Cape Cod,* the four selections of *Maine Woods,* and *A Yankee in Canada* are all, explicitly, travelogues. It is true that, as travelogues, they tend to follow the dictum laid down in *Walden:* "Our Voyaging is only great-circle sailing" (*Walden,* 320). The clearest example is *A Week,* which describes a trip from Concord to Concord to Concord (and perhaps to or at least toward concord). Nor does Thoreau, even while traveling, venture very far; Quebec and Truro are nowhere near as distant as Darwin's Chiloe or Patagonia. But Thoreau, interested in becoming "expert in home-cosmography" (p. 320), is also aware of the advantages to be gained by being a stranger, the man who "has just come out of the woods" and who as a result sees "with unprejudiced senses" that which is misperceived as beautiful only by "the weary traveller, or the returning native—or, perchance, the repentant misanthrope" (*Cape Cod,* 21). Asked to choose between the roles of stranger and native, of traveler and squatter, Thoreau, paradoxically but not surprisingly, wants both.

In Eden, the generalized written record of customary behavior over time—which we usually call history—is out of place, since the blessed condition, as Thoreau defines it, is individual, timeless, and only very approximately describable. The native of Eden, however, still finds natural history useful—as a way of assembling and documenting his case against the unholy world, as a way of finding corroboration for the transcendental moments of elevation and expansion, and as a vehicle for the communication of those moments to the fallen. But Thoreau is not always in Eden; and it will be worthwhile now to observe him when he is far away indeed from the holy place, on his trip to the wrecked world of Cape Cod.

· 6 ·

SUSPECTABLE
REPETITIONS:
CAPE COD

Cape Cod has somehow acquired the reputation of being "Thoreau's sunniest, happiest book"[1] — a reputation attested by the frequency with which copies of the book are to be found in souvenir shops today between Sandwich and Truro. Ironically, the work seems to have become the kind of historical guidebook which Thoreau himself carried along on his excursions to the Cape, in the form of "the eighth volume of the Collections of the Massachusetts Historical Society, printed in 1802" (*Cape Cod*, 20). That Thoreau carried such a book indicates, in a very small way, both the strangeness and unfamiliarity of the place to him, and the degree to which he relies in his account on history of the most traditional kind as a means of understanding this alien land.

The peculiarity of the book's cheery reputation lies in the application of the term "sunny" to a work which begins with a long, and at times painfully detailed description of the immediate aftermath of the wreck of the brig *St. John* (*Cape Cod*, 5–14 and 259), and continues, often in the rain, to see shipwreck at almost every turn. The Cape as a whole, Thoreau imagines, is a potential wreck, preserved only by the most fragile means: "Thus Cape Cod is anchored to the heavens, as it were, by a myriad little cables of beachgrass, and, if they should fail, would become a total wreck, and ere long go to the bottom" (p. 209). Shipwrecks are not, to Thoreau, uniformly disastrous; the visual effect of the *St. John*, for instance, is ambiguous: "I saw that the beauty of the shore itself was wrecked for many a lonely walker there, until he could perceive, at last, how its beauty was enhanced by wrecks like this, and it acquired thus a rarer and sublimer beauty still" (*Cape Cod*, 12). The wrecks serve a very real economic purpose by helping to support the Cape Codders, most of whom work at least part of the time as wreckers or scavengers (pp. 8, 16, 58–59, 116, 162). Thoreau twice mentions the case of "Mr. Bell's nursery" (pp. 115, 166–167), wrecked on board the *Franklin* but thereby spread widely, as the seeds wash ashore. The case seems to Thoreau to be exemplary of a larger, ultimately regenerative, but chillingly (and literally) inhuman process:

> Vessels with seeds in their cargoes, destined for particular ports, where perhaps they were not needed, have been cast away on desolate islands, and though their crews perished, some of their seeds have been preserved. Out of many kinds a few would find a soil and a climate adapted to them, — become naturalized and perhaps drive out the native plants at last, and so fit the land for the habitation of man. It is an ill wind that blows nobody any good, and for the time lamentable shipwrecks may thus contribute a new vegetable to a continent's stock, and prove on the whole a lasting blessing to its inhabitants.   (p. 166)

The reassurance to be found in such speculations rests on, at best, a chastened view of life. The sea, maker of shipwrecks, becomes in Thoreau's eyes an apocalyptic force; as such it is natural in the largest possible sense: "I sympathized rather with the winds and waves, as if to toss and mangle these poor human bodies was the order of the day. If this was the law of Nature, why waste any time in awe or pity? If the last day were come, we should not think so much about the separation of friends or the blighted prospects of individuals" (*Cape Cod*, 11). The wreck of human hopes so evident as Thoreau watches the aftermath of the *St. John* disaster is, from this view, only a sign of the misdirection of those hopes. Is it not possible, he wonders, that "The mariner who makes the safest port in heaven, perchance, seems to his friends on earth to be shipwrecked, for they deem Boston Harbor the better place?" (p. 13). Thoreau, in the end, makes his stand clear; he knows the distance from heaven to Boston, and from heaven to Cape Cod as well: "I wished to see that seashore where man's works are wrecks; to put up at the true Atlantic House, where the ocean is landlord as well as sea-lord, and comes ashore without a wharf for the landing; where the crumbling land is the only invalid, or at best is but dry land, and that is all you can say of it" (p. 65).

At an important moment in *Walden*, Thoreau observes the point at which "the pond asserts its title to a shore, and thus the *shore* is *shorn*" (p. 181). *Cape Cod* is, in a sense, an extended consideration of precisely this kind of landscape, but on an immensely larger scale, and without the comforts to be found on the edge of the pond. Everywhere on the Cape Thoreau finds conflict and flux at the ocean's edge. Near Hull he sees "the sea nibbling voraciously at the continent" (*Cape Cod,* 15) while at the same time making the "wrecks of isles . . . into new shores." "Everything," he notices, "seemed to be gently lapsing into futurity." But the lapse is not always, indeed not usually, so gentle or so well directed. The very edge of the beach takes him back to the primordial time which he glimpsed atop Ktaadn: "Before the land rose out of the ocean, and became dry land, chaos reigned; and between high and low water mark, where she is partially disrobed and rising, a sort of chaos reigns still, which only anomalous creatures can inhabit" (p. 71).

The shore is "a place of wonders" (*Cape Cod,* 174), "a great country" (p. 264), "inexhaustible" in its fertility (p. 120) but also "unfruitful" (p. 122). The beach—that part of the Cape which Thoreau, by choice, makes the scene of almost all of his excursion (pp. 258–259)—is "such a surface as the bottom of the sea made dry land" (p. 25), a world of "naked flesh" (p. 20) constantly being played with by the sea "as a cat plays with a mouse" (p. 155).

A similar confusion of the Empedoclean elements occurs in *Walden,* where the pond is sky-water and a land-lord claiming his title to the shore. Thoreau makes the connection between the sea and smaller bodies of water explicit in *Cape Cod:* "The ocean is but a larger lake" (p. 124). But the possible reassurance to be gained by such an identity of waters is heavily qualified. Elsewhere the connection of sea and pond is assigned to a mistake of perspective, something to be gotten over: "We wished to associate with the ocean until it lost the pond-like look which it wears to a countryman. We still thought we could see the other side" (p. 177). At the same time that Thoreau calls the ocean a lake, he quickly returns to the main line of his argument: "Yet this same placid ocean, as civil now as a city's harbor, a place for ships and commerce, will ere long be lashed into a sudden fury" (p. 125).

He is of course no particular admirer of the civil or of commerce, nor is he likely to be afraid of curative fury. But the pages surrounding Thoreau's equation of the ocean and lake are full of the most violent images of the sea—the mythical Isle of Demons is there, as is a vision of a drowned continent "all livid and frothing at the nostrils, like the body of a drowned man" and of voracious bluefish "slicking" the water by their butchery of other fish, of a storm playing with vessels "like seaweed" and of the sea abusing "the rag of a man's body like the father of mad bulls" (*Cape Cod,* 124–125). Such terrors are not only the mistaken views of Thoreau the inlander; he debunks the notion that "they who have been long conversant with the ocean can foretell" and thus survive its violence—"probably no such ancient mariner exists" (p. 126).

The confusion of earth, air, and water in *Walden* is a sign of redemptive transformation, of mediation, of Eden. The chaos where earth, air, and water meet on Cape Cod is, by contrast, a place of devastation, an earthly hell. The sea may, momentarily, take on the calm aspect of a lake; but its nature is anything but calm. At the top of Ktaadn Thoreau had seen a nature with no relation to man; in the sea he finds a nature whose only human relation is one of threat and outright destruction. It is terrible even when calm:

> Though there were numerous vessels at this great distance in the horizon on every side, yet the vast spaces between them, like the spaces between the stars—far as they were distant from us, so were they from one another—nay, some were twice as far from each other as from us,—impressed us with a sense of the immensity of the ocean, the "unfruitful ocean," as it has been called, and we could see what proportion man and his works bear to the globe. As we looked off, and saw the water growing darker and darker and deeper and deeper the farther we looked, till it was awful to consider, and it appeared to have no relation to the friendly land, either as shore or bottom,—of what use is a bottom if it is out of sight, if it is two or three miles from the surface, and you are to be drowned so long before you get to it, though it were made of the same stuff with your native soil?—over that ocean where, as the Veda says, "there is nothing to give support, nothing to rest upon, nothing to cling to," I felt that I was a land animal. (*Cape Cod,* 122–123)

The faith that the naturalist-mystic brought to *Walden*—"let us settle ourselves . . . till we come to hard bottom and rocks in place, which we can call *reality,* and say, This is and no mistake" (*Walden,* 97–98)—will not suffice at Truro. Thoreau has attained what he set out after—"to get a better view than I had yet had of the ocean" (*Cape Cod,* 3)—only to find it an awful thing.

One clue as to why the vision is so awful can be found in Thoreau's closing remarks. Like any good guide, he offers to the tourist some practical advice—where to go, where to stay, and, most significant of all, when to visit:

> Most persons visit the seaside in warm weather . . . But I suspect that the fall is the best season, for then the atmosphere is more transparent, and it is a greater pleasure to look out over the sea. The clear and bracing air, and the storms of autumn, and winter even, are necessary in order that we may get the impression which the sea is calculated to make. In October, when the weather is not intolerably cold, and the landscape wears its autumnal tints, such as, methinks, only a Cape Cod landscape ever wears, especially if you have a storm during your stay,—that I am convinced is the best time to visit this shore. (*Cape Cod,* 272)

Walden Pond was a perennial spring; the Cape is a landscape of fall, and, applying one of Thoreau's favorite puns, of the Fall. The shore of the vast ocean is the place where, even more clearly than in benighted Concord, men suffer the curse of the Expulsion—cursed land bringing forth sea grass as its own thorn and thistle, cursed sweating labor of the harshest kind, ending only in sudden and inevitable death. The Cape Codders scrabbling for a living from the remains of battered vessels are indeed the fallen; and they are, Thoreau notices, terribly like all the rest of us (*Cape Cod,* 115): "Are we not all wreckers contriving that some treasure may be washed up on our beach?" But what is to be found in "the waste and wrecks of human art" thus "vomited up" by the sea is more often a corpse or a piece of half-rotted rope or a bottle of red ale than a treasure.

Cape Cod, to Thoreau, appears then as a polar opposite of Walden, a damp grey littered Inferno in contrast to the paradisal spot near Concord. History found little place in that paradise; but hell, as it turns out, is for Thoreau the perfect place to show the applicability, however limited, of the old authorities. Most frequently, history in *Cape Cod* is the record of decay, and the means of seeing all the more clearly the continuing decline of human endeavor in this unregenerate land. He approaches, for example, the village of Sandwich by way of his volume of Historical Collections, only to find that the place is sadly disappointing: "Ours was but half a Sandwich at most, and that must have fallen on the buttered side some time" (*Cape Cod,* 21). He discovers, as further evidence of the poor condition of the villagers, clear sign of that overdeveloped respect for the customs and ways of the past which is the dark, entrapping side of a sense of history. The book tells him that: "The inhabitants of Sandwich generally manifest a fond and steady adherence to the manners, employments, and modes of living which characterized their fathers." To which Thoreau adds the observation that this "made me think that they were, after all, very much like all the rest of the world" (p. 22). Much later, in Truro, Thoreau again consults his authorities for evidence of the industry, supposedly once prosperous there, of raising sheep. All Thoreau can find when he visits is one cow "tethered in the desert" and he comments that "the country looked so barren that I several times refrained from asking the inhabitants for a string or a piece of paper, for fear that I should rob them" (p. 139).[2] Taken at face value, the "authoritative" records of the past show all the more clearly how barren the Cape is in Thoreau's present, and how much of the blame the inhabitants must bear for the decline.

It is a reversal of his usual method: the observable present is tested against the recorded past, and not vice-versa. If the angle of vision is reversed, the question arises, as we shall see, of whether the authorities are reliable, since, measured against the hard reality of Cape Cod as Thoreau sees it, they are consistently wrong. The reasonable approach to the problem is a suspicious attitude; finding, in one case, a continuity of report from past and present, and one asserting the fertility even today of the Cape, Thoreau observes: "The recent accounts are in some instances *suspectable repetitions* of the old, and I have no doubt that their statements are as often founded on the exception as the rule, and that by far the greater number of acres are as barren as they appear to be" (*Cape Cod*, 39; my italics). That is the more usual, and more reliable, appeal—from account to observation. The recent statements are doubly suspect—because they are repetitious of old and questionable documents, and because they are at variance with the appearance of things now. Thoreau finds, on further investigation, that historical accounts generally are often also "suspectable repetitions," and as such must be used warily. The one historical fact that seems to hold true continuously on Cape Cod is the sad and meaningful prevalence of shipwreck. The Cape is indeed, and has always been, that shore where man's works and hopes are wrecked.

ARMED, however ineffectually, with his guidebook and prepared for his encounter with the grim facts of Cape Cod life by his observation of the wreckage where the *St. John* had foundered, Thoreau sets off on his trip to the sea. He presents the trip as a continuation of his earlier ventures, which had lead to *Walden:* "I have been accustomed to make excursions to the ponds within ten miles of Concord, but latterly I extended my excursions to the seashore" (*Cape Cod,* 3). But by traveling so far from Concord, he encounters the problem of perspective.

In *Walden,* we remember, he had insisted that the fundamental act was settling, not traveling. He had dismissed the second-hand accounts of travelers (*Walden,* 211) and had missed no opportunity to point out the futility of those who travel in search of wealth or peace (pp. 92 and 320–322). One sign of his superiority to John Field is that Thoreau "had sat there [where Field now lives] many times of old before the ship was built that floated his family to America" (p. 204). The issue seems clearly drawn; it is the native, the deliberately still and settled man who can best front the essential facts.

In *Cape Cod* Thoreau is a stranger. He acknowledges in the very first sentence that the ocean, to one "who lives even a few miles inland," is "another world" (*Cape Cod,* 3). His effort to overcome his own ignorance of the sea is represented not by settling on its shore but by wandering on the beach, moving almost continuously. Now it is the stranger to whom he gives the advantage: "A stranger may easily detect what is strange to the oldest inhabitant, for the strange is his province" (p. 192). Repeatedly he reminds his readers that he is an "inlander," a landsman, a "countryman" (pp. 34, 41, 65, 68, 123). The freshness of observation which a traveler may bring has its clear advantages—the natives, dulled by familiarity, miss entirely the "inspiriting sound" of the sea roar (p. 40). The inlander is frequently subject to mistakes of vision—"Indeed, to an inlander, the Cape landscape is a constant mirage" (p. 41)—but that is, to Thoreau, no conclusive drawback.

In fact, the confusion may be productive of fable and myth. It is the landsman's confusion which, in part, allows at the seashore "the animal and vegetable kingdoms" to be "strangely mingled" (*Cape Cod,* 68). Even the more foolish errors which a traveler makes have their beneficial effects. Thoreau visits the Shank-Painter Swamp only because "as a landsman naturally would" he misunderstands the name and expects something colorful (p. 200). Instead, he finds a wealth of natural history on the way—spiders, beach grass, tortoises, toads, and strawberries. And in the end the trip is Transcendentally rewarding as well. The landscape he sees en route to the swamp is "the dreariest scenery imaginable" (p. 201), but then he is not interested in mere scenery. In the desert there he finds more evidence of the peculiar nature of the Cape, the dead remains of what had been a flourishing forest (p. 203), signs of "inundations" and evidence of the continuing strife of the shore, with the operative force being an especially concise union of the elements—"a tide of sand impelled by waves and wind" (p. 204). The trip culminates in Thoreau's realization of the Cape's fragile moorings, which I have already quoted: "This Cape Cod is anchored to the heavens, as it were, by a myriad little cables of beach grass" (p. 209).

There are more mundane advantages. Only because he is a stranger, and thus unlikely to return and make use of the information, Thoreau is shown "the best locality for strawberries" (*Cape Cod,* 203) and, ironically, is given some information about the location of the only substantial rock near Eastham, which, by its rarity, had acquired a peculiar value to the natives, "equal to a transfer of California 'rocks,' almost" (pp. 223–224). The two instances provide a useful key to the mixed nature of the natives. Their knowledge of strawberries is undoubtedly to be admired; we remember Thoreau's own fondness for berries on Fair Haven Hill, and his insistence that only the man who picks and eats them knows fruit truly (*Walden,* 173). But Thoreau the traveler is particularly equipped to see the foolishness of the Cape Codders' misplaced interest in rocks, since he has visited such rocky places as Cohasset and Marblehead (*Cape Cod,* 225). It is this breadth of comparative knowledge which constitutes the stranger's advantage over the native (unless, like Thoreau, the native is also a traveler). Any one fact, as we are told in *Walden* and as such incidents in *Cape Cod* as the discovery of the ale bottle (p. 117) re-emphasize, can yield a sense of the whole if Transcendentally viewed. Or so, at least, can the essential facts. But how is one to know the essential? We remember that the task of accumulating, sorting, and assessing is fundamental to the natural historian; it is, as we shall see, equally fundamental to the kind of historiography Thoreau undertakes in his chapter on Provincetown. Natural history (in its written form), travelogue, and history are to the reader what travel is to the first-hand observer: a way of assembling the range of knowledge necessary to counterweigh the possible misdirection of a more narrow and deliberate vision; a way of knowing the uniqueness of Walden to be true and the uniqueness of Eastham rock to be false.

The natives whom Thoreau encounters on Cape Cod (and of course

the majority of those settled in and around Concord) are brave enough
(as was John Field), but not especially percipient. Thoreau's well-
known dialogue with the Wellfleet Oysterman is a small exemplary
summary of the generality of his meetings with the natives. The
Oysterman is a curious mixture of ignorance and knowledge. He
knows about the Concord Fight but not precisely where Concord is
(*Cape Cod*, 80–81) and knows his Bible but speaks well of it only out
of "prudence," not faith (p. 82). His trade, while providing him a
"competency," is yet another declining Cape industry—the native
oysters have died out and the business continues now only by import-
ing stock from the south (pp. 82–83). Even about oysters he has less
than complete knowledge. He insists that oysters can move only "just
as much as my shoe," which Thoreau the naturalist knows is not
necessarily the case. The Oysterman knows the names of ponds—
surely an important skill to Thoreau—and of vegetables (pp. 98–100)
but has some trouble recalling his wife's name (p. 95) and his days as a
pilot have passed because "now they had changed the names so he
might be bothered" (p. 90). The Oysterman's first-hand knowledge of
history serves to Thoreau the useful purpose of corroborating written
records (p. 92), and, being a man of the sea, the Oysterman is especially well informed about shipwrecks.

Between Thoreau the inland traveler and the native shore-living
Oysterman, things end more or less in a standoff. The traveler's
freshness of experience (the Oysterman thinks it is simple ignorance)
allows him to taste the "sweet and savory" sea clam (*Cape Cod*, 73)
and to handle the sun-squall (pp. 86–87)—an opportunity Thoreau
would not have wanted to miss, if only for its potential as a mystical
pun. The Oysterman explains (p. 86) that the clam is partly poisonous
and the sun-squall noxious to handle, which in turn allows Thoreau to
feel noticeably superior (and unusually tactful); as for the clam, "I did
not tell him that I had eaten a large one entire that afternoon, but
began to think that I was tougher than a cat." The pride passes
away—"In the course of the evening I began to feel the potency of the
clam which I had eaten . . . I was made quite sick by it for a short
time while [the Oysterman] laughed at my expense" (p. 94). His only
consolation is to find in *Mourt's Relation* an account of the same error—and the same illness—among the Pilgrims. So much, at any rate,
for the absolute virtue of the unmediated experience of Nature; there
is at least some advice "from my seniors" which, *pace Walden*, Thoreau

might profitably have listened to (*Walden,* 9). On the other hand, the wariness based on custom, which is characteristic of the Oysterman, is no more absolutely reliable; Thoreau suffers not an itch from the "poisonous" sun-squall.

What Thoreau settles upon, then, is not an unequivocal preference for either strangers or natives, but a kind of synthesis which approximates "neutral ground," a way of seeing that is neither parochial (in the negative sense) nor superficial. This angle of vision is a beneficial effect of Thoreau's visit to the awful seaside:

> The seashore is a sort of neutral ground, a most advantageous point from which to contemplate this world. It is even a trivial place. The waves forever rolling to the land are too far-travelled and untamable to be familiar . . . It is a wild, rank place, and there is no flattery in it. Strewn with crabs, horseshoes, and razor clams, and whatever the sea casts up, — a vast *morgue,* where famished dogs may range in packs, and crows come daily to glean the pittance which the tide leaves them. The carcasses of men and beasts together lie stately up upon its shelf, rotting and bleaching in the sun and waves, and each tide turns them in their beds, and tucks fresh sand under them. There is naked nature, — inhumanly sincere, wasting no thought on man, nibbling at the cliffy shore where gulls wheel amid the spray. (*Cape Cod,* 186)

The value Thoreau finds is not objectivity; in a journal entry of May 6, 1854, Thoreau insists that "there is no such thing as a pure *objective* observation" (*Journal,* VI, 236). He goes on to raise again the issue of travel: "It matters not where or how far you travel, — the farther commonly the worse, — but how much alive you are." Or, we might say, it matters not where you travel but how, as it matters not where but how you settle. The peculiar experience of Cape Cod is that it allows Thoreau to be especially alive to and in a landscape that is a morgue, a collection of mementos of death and of the vanity of earthly hope.

But even in that landscape Thoreau finds his moments of insight. One of the most important occurs in the chapter devoted to "The Beach." Thoreau seeks out a "charity house," a shelter set up for the care of shipwrecked sailors. Putting his eye to "a knot-hole in the door" he sees more than a derelict building:

> After long looking without seeing, into the dark, — not knowing how many shipwrecked men's bones we might see at last, looking with the eye of faith, knowing that, though to him that knocketh it may not

always be opened, yet to him that looketh long enough through a knot-hole the inside shall be visible, — for we had had some practice at looking inward, — by steadily keeping our other ball covered from the light meanwhile, putting the outward world behind us, ocean and land, and the beach, — till the pupil became enlarged and collected the rays of light that were wandering in that dark (for the pupil shall be enlarged by looking; there never was so dark a night but a faithful and patient eye, however small, might at last prevail over it) — after all this, I say, things began to take shape in our vision, — if we may use this expression where there was nothing but emptiness, — and we obtained the long-wished-for insight.   (*Cape Cod*, 76–77)

It is Thoreau's most clever answer to his own question — will you be a student merely or a seer? Be a pupil and you are at the same moment both student and see-er. It is the moment he went to the Cape for, or at least a moment he went to the Cape to rediscover, another chance to "link my facts to my fable" (*Walden*, 184). Notice how easily the scientific fact of the enlargement of the pupil of the eye becomes a symbolic pun. Thoreau is once again writing a new scripture, in part by turning the old Scripture inside out; he revises the familiar words of Matthew VII:7 in a subordinate clause. He identifies this vision — which, like a good mystic, he is not sure he has the power to express — with the sense of apocalyptic threat he finds elsewhere on the edge of the sea; he is "at last, looking with the eye of faith." He shows that he has learned the chastening lesson of this purgatory, by putting the outward world behind him. His final words in *Cape Cod* are an extension of this — "A man may stand there and put all America behind him" (*Cape Cod*, 273).

It appears at first, however, that all this complexity of syntax and allusion amounts to a Transcendental shaggy-dog story; for what Thoreau sees, after identifying himself with the "blind bard" Milton, is a chimney, "some stones and some loose wads of wool on the floor, and an empty fireplace at the further end" (*Cape Cod*, 77) — hardly worth putting aside the world for. But this is only the visible, in the mundane sense; he had rebuked, in his journal, those who "take cognizance of outward things merely" (*Journal*, VI, 236–237; 6 May 1854). The real vision, the "long-wished-for insight"[3] constitutes yet another proof of the bitter lessons of the whole excursion: "Turning our backs on the outward world, we thus looked through the knot-hole into the Humane house, into the very bowels of mercy; and for bread we found a stone . . . This, then, is what charity hides! Virtues antique and far away, with ever a rusty nail over the latch; and very difficult to keep in repair, withal, it is so uncertain whether any will ever gain the beach near you" (*Cape Cod*, 78). As Thoreau remarks at the end of the chapter, a few sentences later, "I did not intend this for a sentimental journey" (p. 78), and indeed it is not. But if this is where he ends, where did he begin? His conclusion is to put behind him all outward things; but he finds the site of this inward vision by a long wandering in the out-of-doors.

More literally, the chapter which ends at the charity house consists primarily, up until its final pages, of natural history and antiquarianism. Thoreau spends some time observing wreckers (*Cape Cod*, 59–60), naturalizing man, as he had done in "The Village." He discusses, with appropriate citations, the uses and nature of driftwood (pp. 60–61); he observes and describes the topography of the beach (pp. 61–64). He finds the time to record "a remarkable method of catching gulls, derived from the Indians" (p. 71) and to read, apparently in " 'Description of the Eastern Coast of the County of Barnstable,' printed in 1802" (p. 63), about the habits and names of gulls (p. 72). In the end, he is directed to the charity house into which he looks so productively by the same "authority" that explains the function of the houses and gives him detailed instruction about where they are to be found (pp. 74–76).

We have here, again, a gathering of the ways in which the world's methods and the world's authorities may be used by the man seeking a kind of "insight and far-sight" (*Walden*, 288) which is normally beyond the reach of scientist or historian, and which may depend upon turning one's back on the world. By going over the ground with the eye of the naturalist and with the range of information to be gained from historical accounts, Thoreau finds the place where insight occurs.

BLESSED MEN, Thoreau loves to remind us, have no need of history. But on Cape Cod Thoreau can find his blessedness only in the negative, in his estrangement from the purgatorial world of sand, wind, ocean, beach grass, and wreckage. There, history is not only relevant, it is inescapable. Thoreau carries it with him, in the form of his historical guidebook and his knowledge of the early chroniclers of the New World: Thomas Morton, Edward Winslow, John Smith, Beverly, William Wood. The records of the past are there in any case, in the Truro graveyard (*Cape Cod*, 159) or in the relics, human and otherwise, on the beaches (p. 107). And there is the constant sea, with which "we do not associate the idea of antiquity" (pp. 188–189) since it changes not at all over time, but whose ominous timelessness makes the records of human time all the more noticeable, and all the more pitiable.

In this time-bound, relic-strewn, fallen world, Thoreau finds the occasion to undertake his most extended historical investigations: the ecclesiastical history of Eastham (*Cape Cod*, 43–56), and the attempt to find in all written records the true discoverer of Cape Cod (pp. 226–257). The two are exemplary, indeed monitory histories. And they are set in a context of a more general consideration of the role and value of history. We remember Thoreau's comments about "suspectable repetitions." But Thoreau's affection for old accounts—"I love to quote so good authority" (*Week*, 5)—is apparent. Indeed, repetition is, in its way, a virtue, as is the eye for detail he finds in the old books: "The old accounts are the richest in topography, which was what we wanted most; and, indeed, in most things else, for I find that the readable parts of the modern accounts of these towns consist, in a great measure, of quotations, acknowledged and unacknowledged, from the older ones, without any other information of equal interest" (*Cape Cod*, 42). By reading the old accounts for their topography, Thoreau again uses them, not for their own, but for his purposes. History, properly read, need not be read on the authors' terms.

No account is truly satisfactory. As in *The Maine Woods* the particular evidence of this is to be found in maps, but Thoreau generalizes the point: "[Cape Cod] was not as on the map, or seen from the stage coach; but there I found it all out of doors, huge and real, Cape Cod! as it cannot be represented on a map, color it as you will; the thing itself, than which there is nothing more like it, no truer picture or account" (*Cape Cod*, 65). Thoreau indulges himself at one point by recording a more blunt rejection of accounts (" 'Damn book-peddlars,—all the time talking about books. Better do something. Damn 'em. I'll shoot 'em' "—p. 90) but those are only the mutterings of the Oysterman's "fool." In a more serious way, Thoreau raises again the point that time, pursued back far enough, defeats itself. Quoting a Swiss colleague of Agassiz, Édouard Desor, he argues that " 'in going back through the geological ages, we come to an epoch when, according to all appearances, the dry land did not exist, and when the surface of our globe was entirely covered with water' " (p. 128) which is, as he has asserted elsewhere, the most timeless of elements.

The decline from myth to history to the sketchy records of modern life is a sign of the more general decline from ancient and heroic times. Speaking of the difficult voyage of a Cape Cod sea captain, Thoreau claims that: "In ancient times the adventures of these two or three men and boys would have been made the basis of a myth, but now such tales are crowded into a line of shorthand signs, like an algebraic formula in the shipping news" (*Cape Cod*, 141). Compared to the newspapers, history is better. But its limitations are sharply delineated: useful not for its own ends, below myth in ultimate value, and subject to the test of current observation, always to be known as questionable and second-hand.

Why then use it at all? Having told the tale of the Wellfleet Oysterman, Thoreau asks, "*Quid loquar?* Why repeat what he told us?" (*Cape Cod*, 94). His answer is to quote Virgil's *Eclogue VI*, where the poet asks the same question concerning the songs of Silenus.[4] The answer is, in the immediate sense, no answer at all; Thoreau replies to his own question by quoting Virgil's. The passage mentions the story of Scylla, who tore apart sailors in the depths of the sea—a monster still likely inhabiting the ocean off Cape Cod. The Virgilian parallel at least implies that the Oysterman's history (he has been telling about his memories of George Washington) is of value as myth and as literature, if not as fact.

And history is a tonic against idleness. Thoreau introduces his survey of the history of Eastham by suggesting it will pass the time: "As it will take us an hour to get over this plain, and there is no variety in the prospect, peculiar as it is, I will read a little in the history of Eastham the while" (*Cape Cod*, 42–43). Although it soon appears this is more than a pastime, we have been warned not to expect anything too lively. Thoreau has, on the previous page, provided a short, sour, but accurate *precis* of such histories: a matter of pastors, old prayers, and ecclesiastical councils (p. 42).

Thoreau begins, however, with an issue of more import than ecclesiastical councils, and one of wider application than Eastham. The town, he records, was acquired in small part by purchase, in larger part simply by claiming that "Not Any" other being owned the lands taken by settlers: "Perhaps this was the first instance of that quiet way of 'speaking for' a place not yet occupied, or at least not improved as much as it may be, which their descendants have practiced, and are still practicing so extensively" (*Cape Cod*, 43). Finding, in the case of Eastham, an Indian, Lieutenant Anthony, who years later appeared, claimed, and received payment for lands north of Eastham, Thoreau wonders if a similar event may take place "at the door of the White House some day" — perhaps as repayment for the dispossession of the Cherokee. But it is not only a matter of mistreatment of the natives, or a reminder that the natives he encounters on the Cape are in fact not so native as they seem. There is a larger point, a contributory explanation of why this place is the home of the damned: "I know that if you hold a thing unjustly, there will surely be the devil to pay at last" (p. 43).

Having established the shoddy foundation of the town, Thoreau mounts an anecdotal survey of the early religious history of Eastham. As one might expect, he misses few opportunities to see the shallowness and misdirection of the religious practices he observes. The overall intent of the survey is, first of all, to identify the self-deluding and even hysterical roots of Eastham's ecclesiastical establishment. Thoreau does this good-humoredly and at a distance; he makes few references to contemporary practices of the more widely accepted sort, and thus he avoids directly offending his readers. He does tell about camp meetings which are, unmistakeably but quietly, identified as conventions of lunatics: "They select a time for their meetings when the moon is full" (*Cape Cod*, 48). Few of the readers of *Putnam's Weekly* were likely to take offense at the ridicule of religious extremism; Thoreau will not, however, allow his readers wholly to escape the brunt of his charge simply by separating themselves, as most would do willingly, from the more extravagant and declassé religious enthusiasms. Acknowledging his own inability to follow the complications of doctrine in one case he recounts, Thoreau falls back on a vague but pointed summary: "And many the like distinctions they made, such as some of my readers, probably, are more familiar with than I am" (pp. 53–54). Eastham is, after all, one example of the Puritan roots of the general moral polity of New England in Thoreau's time; if the proud parishoners of early Cape Cod are misguided, are not their descendants equally so?

Thoreau softens the case by admitting that Cape Cod is a unique place: "We conjectured that the reason for the perhaps unusual, if not unhealthful development of the religious sentiment here, was the fact that a large portion of the population are women whose husbands and sons are either abroad on the sea, or else drowned, and there is nobody but they and the ministers left behind" (*Cape Cod*, 46). The effects are hysterical and dehumanizing. Thoreau finds one "singularly masculine woman" who escapes madness only at the price of any sort of human feeling; she is "hard enough for any enormity" (p. 47). These are not, we must suppose, peculiar accidents—they are only "*perhaps unusual*"—but rather the direct result of the misdirection of spirit Thoreau finds in Puritan religion. It is yet another explanation of why the Cape is a place of spiritual death, producing, by way of art, no more than commendatory occasional verses on the fall of Governor Prence's pear tree, which Thoreau can bear to quote only in part (pp. 43–44). By recounting the very events which the settlers took enough pride in to record, Thoreau manages to show how little they lived "an Achillean life" (p. 45). He uses the history of the place against itself: by your own chronicles shall ye be judged.

The case of Reverend Samuel Osborn (*Cape Cod*, 52–54) shows this.[5] Osborn, accused of having "embraced the religion of Arminius," is tried and found inadequate by "an ecclesiastical council consisting of ministers" which—a lovely pun—"sat upon him, and . . . naturally enough, spoiled his usefulness." Osborn is dismissed and moves to Boston to keep a school. But, alone among the clergy Thoreau mentions, Osborn was indeed useful, and in the practical way of which Thoreau is completely approving. He "taught his people the use of peat, and the art of drying and preparing it, which, as they had scarcely any other fuel, was a great blessing to them." In addition he was an agriculturalist. Such usefulness is no defense against a sitting council. Thoreau observes, knowingly using the language of a doctrine which is fundamental (and fundamentally in *error*) according to the fathers of Protestantism, that Osborn "was fully justified, methinks, by his works in the peat meadow." Had there been more hewing of peat and hoeing of beans, and less preaching of the sort which Thoreau quotes at length (pp. 49–50), both the crops and the spirit of the Cape might be less barren.

Thoreau, at the last, seems to turn aside his wrath, in a passage which is a fine example of damnation disguised as courtesy: "Let no one think that I do not love the old ministers. They were, probably, the best men of their generation, and they deserve that their biographies should fill the pages of the town histories" (*Cape Cod*, 55). This, of men who frighten "comparatively innocent" young men "nearly out of [their] wits" (p. 51), and who, apparently, cannot tell Latin from Nipmuck (p. 55): if such are the best, what of the commonality?

In "Provincetown" the Pilgrims are examined more extensively, and somewhat less antagonistically, as possible exemplars of the properly deliberate life. Here Thoreau indulges in a sort of criticism of the New England foundation[6] which we have in the twentieth century come to accept as stereotypically correct. He makes his point, as later critics have done, by using the settlers' own historical account against them. He does not, we notice, question the accuracy of these accounts, perhaps because, as in the case of Millennium Grove meeting-ground and the murderous Nauset woman (*Cape Cod,* 47–48), he finds ample corroboration within the sight of his own eyes. What he does is to define, in the words of the damned, the elements of the damnation he sees, and to show how, properly read, history may have a salutary effect utterly opposed to the intentions of its writers.

The pages (*Cape Cod,* 225–257) which Thoreau devotes in his "Provincetown" chapter to the question of who first and best explored Cape Cod offer a more complex example of Thoreau as historian. Here he addresses directly the question of the comparative validity of sources. His basic tests, not surprisingly, are language (especially the language of naming) and geographic detail. His effort is not so single-mindedly condemnatory as it was in his survey of Eastham. Now he tries to find not only examples of delusion and failure, but exemplary lives in the positive sense. The moment of discovery is not, to him, a time of purely historical interest; could he find in the record of the past a detailed account of true discovery, he might better be able to recognize and to describe his own attempt always to live in an attitude of discovery. Failing that, he can see in the record of repeated discovery and rediscovery a type of the kind of self-renewing Transcendental holiness which he hopes to make the fundamental element of his life: "If America was found and lost again, as most of us believe [and as his documents seem to prove], then why not twice? especially as there were likely to be so few records of an earlier discovery. Consider what stuff history is made of, — that for the most part it is merely a story agreed upon by posterity . . . I believe that, if I were to live the life of mankind over again myself (which I would not be hired to do[7]), with the Universal History in my hands, I should not be able to tell what was what" (p. 250).

As with science, Thoreau is always aware of the potential hazards of his mode of inquiry; the acquisition of more knowledge is less preferable than the acquisition of better knowledge. More information might only lead to the kind of entrapment in detail which Thoreau lamented in his journal. With that in mind, he shifts his ground, working deep rather than broad, and considers at length the Pilgrims, "discoverers" at least in the common legend. Thoreau can, in studying them, consider exactly what the nature of discovery and its potential failures are. It is very much to his taste to find an example of failure; if earlier discoverers have, in some recognizable way, missed their chance, it leaves the field open to Thoreau himself, to be not merely a rediscoverer but a true discoverer. For a man convinced of the value of individuality and originality, the distinction is by no means unimportant.

It is a question of naming which begins Thoreau's venture backwards. He notices how "on successive maps, Cape Cod appears sprinkled over with French, Dutch, and English names, as it made part of New France, New Holland, and New England" (*Cape Cod,* 226). That leads, in its turn, to the larger question of exploration, and to the first of Thoreau's historiographic points: "It is remarkable that there is not in English any adequate or correct account of the French exploration of what is now the coast of New England, between 1604 and 1608" (p. 227). Such an account does exist in French, and constitutes "the most interesting chapter of what we may call the ante-Pilgrim history of New England" (p. 228). Thoreau goes on to show both the general ignorance, on the part of English and American historians, of this account in its full form, and the frequent unacknowledged use—indeed, copying—of portions of the French account by these same English and American authorities (pp. 228–229). He spends some time asserting the priority and the extent of the French experience in New England (pp. 230–237). In passing he raises again the issue of "just title" (p. 233) and points out how, by comparison with the French, the English settlers show a sad inability to derive adequate information even from those things they should have known first-hand (p. 236). Here is one major theme of Thoreau's historical excursion: the measurement of the Pilgrim experience against that of the French. It is the French, and especially Champlain, who seem, at first, to win the contest.

But at least on the point of priority, even the French are inadequate, as Thoreau shows by citing the history, before Champlain, of visits to "this country of 'Norumbega' " (*Cape Cod,* 238–247), including an extended description of the moment when "Cape Cod is commonly said to have been discovered in 1602" by Bartholomew Gosnold (pp. 246–247). The problem with this legendary discovery, as Thoreau demonstrates, is its vagueness, especially when tested against the standard of detail and accuracy represented by Champlain's *Voyages*. The story as Thoreau tells it is full of errors of judgment (Gosnold at first mistakes the "savages" for "Christians distressed," p. 243), and there is plenty of evidence that Gosnold was not the first to visit these shores. One of the savages he meets comes dressed, roughly, as an Englishman (pp. 243–244). There are also repeated mistakes of language (the aborigines are, in the words of the chronicler, able "to understand much more than we . . . for want of language, could comprehend," p. 244) and failures of naming. Most of Gosnold's names for the features he "discovered" do not remain in use (p. 247).

Thus weak on the face of it, the case of Gosnold proves susceptible to attack on another front: consulting "old Icelandic manuscripts" Thoreau raises the possibility of visits by the "hardy race" of Northmen (*Cape Cod,* 247–249), as well as "the claims of several other worthy persons" (pp. 249–251). The Northmen are particularly of interest to him, since they allow Thoreau to name himself as the true discoverer. The possible first visitors he names—Thor-finn, Thorwald—share with Thoreau the same initial syllable. One of them "is said to have had a son born in New England" (p. 248). Explicitly, that son was the ancestor of "Thorwaldson the sculptor." But implicitly it is Thoreau himself. Some pages before, discussing a mirage he sees in Truro, Thoreau made the connection directly: "But whether Thorfinn saw the mirage here or not, Thor-eau, one of the same family, did; and perchance it was because Leif the Lucky had, in a previous voyage, taken Thor-er and his people off the rock in the middle of the sea, that Thor-eau was born to see it" (p. 192).

The overall effect of Thoreau's researches is twofold. First, it emphasizes the recurrence of discovery; second, it makes it clear that it was Thoreau himself who was "born to see it" truly for the first time. The point is not so much, after all, the priority as the *quality* of discovery; and to investigate that Thoreau devotes himself to the most familiar case, that of the Pilgrims who landed in Provincetown Harbor "on the 11th of November, 1620, old style" (*Cape Cod,* 251–257). Using their own chronicle, the misnamed *Mourt's Relation,*[8] he considers their strengths and weaknesses as discoverers, and as models for his own exploratory excursion. It is the clearest example of Thoreau using the method of the naturalist to assess the validity of a historical authority. Thoreau tests each element of the account in *Mourt's Relation* against the observations he himself makes. The Pilgrims are correct about the shallowness of the harbor (pp. 251–252), but wrong in most other ways. At least Thoreau can find no corroboration for what the chronicle says about fowl, wood, soil, and vegetation.

It is a troublesome point. The fault could be one of inaccuracy of the chronicle, or yet another sign of the progressive decline of the Cape since the arrival of the profaning hand of man: "All accounts agree in affirming that this part of the Cape was comparatively well wooded a century ago. But notwithstanding the great changes which have taken place in these respects, I cannot but think that we must make some allowance for the greenness of the Pilgrims in these matters, which caused them to see green . . . Their account may be true particularly, but it is generally false" (*Cape Cod,* 255). This is, if you will, the obverse of the necessary and virtuous subjectivity of observation which Thoreau asserts in his journal entry of May 6, 1854. And it serves to complicate further the balance between strangers and natives; here are strangers who bring not insight but preconception to their observation.

In the end, the Pilgrims will not serve as adequate models of discovery—"they possessed but few of the qualities of the modern pioneer" (*Cape Cod,* 256). This is due in large part to their refusal to act as individuals—"they were a family and a church, and were more anxious to keep together, though it were on the sand, than to explore and colonize a New World" (p. 256). The connection to those who sit in Concord reading newspapers or the riders on the Iron Horse who barely find the time to glance at Walden Pond is clear. Again Thoreau invokes the example of Champlain; he, in the same circumstances, "would have sought an interview with the savages, and examined the country as far as the Connecticut, and made a map of it, before Billington had climed his tree" (p. 257).[9] It is Champlain who leaves behind him "a minute and faithful account" (p. 237). While the English "fable"—in this case, not a useful occupation—Champlain acts, bringing to the task the virtues of the naturalist, and of Thoreau at Walden, "measuring and sounding" (p. 236). Champlain, too, is imperfect; he is French, for one thing, and decidedly unfriendly to the Indians (p. 237). But he shows what a man of action and of observation might do.

This search for exemplary predecessors is a further and important use to which Thoreau puts history. It is a task of peculiar significance, and peculiar difficulty, to the American saint (a genus of which Thoreau and Whitman are representative). The very hope of finding full-scale examples in the past is, in its way, a denial of one's own sainthood, since holiness in the New World style is inherently unique and individual. The true American saint can have no predecessor, no model after which to pattern his life. Necessarily, his only hero is the self. It is for this reason that the exemplars he finds are, most commonly, obscure and failures. Their obscurity insures that they do not represent the weight of custom which the American saint hopes to avoid; were they less eccentric, posterity would have agreed to remember them as a part of received history. Their failure serves the purposes of allowing the saint to retain his originality while deriving the reassurance that the task is worthy. So too does the saint's choice of exemplary figures whose explicit action is unlike his own; Columbus' voyage is vastly different from Thoreau's.

But the search for usable predecessors goes on. History serves the purpose, then, of proving that the discovery of "the only true America" is an old and esteemed goal, and that it has never quite been done. So it remains a prospect worth the most intense effort. With that knowledge one may face with some serenity even the ominous and inhumanely sincere ocean, with all America behind him, knowing that he faces yet another wilderness with another, truer America yet to be found.

CONCLUSION:
SORTING
THE RUBBLE

THOREAU as historian follows his own prescription; he does not attempt to present the past. His survey of the history of Eastham takes the form, not of re-creation or true narrative, but of commentary. He continually cites his sources, not out of a sense of scholarly protocol, but to remind the reader of the ineradicable distance between the past and present, between the authority and the careful reader. That distance is essential; but the awareness of it does not constitute a full repudiation of history or of the accumulation of second-hand knowledge generally.

History is to Thoreau useful if not presentable—a phrase which fits, as well, the character of the crotchety surveyor he adopts as his own in "The Succession of Forest Trees" and elsewhere. History is a source of context and corroboration, a standard of measurement as useful, in its own way, as a notched stick or a plumbline. What is most effectively measured by history is the degree to which man has fallen, the distance which he must traverse to reach Transcendental sainthood. The nearer one approaches that blessed state, the nearer one comes, that is, to the end of the rainbow or to the bottom of Walden Pond, the less important this standard of measurement becomes—as indeed is true of all of the world's standards and disciplines. This is why the prevalence of historical matter is greater in those works, particularly *A Week* and *Cape Cod,* in which Thoreau is away from his holy place. Going over the ground in Purgatory, Thoreau takes a historical guidebook; he needs no books but his Homer in the shack by the pond.

Thoreau uses history, as we have seen, in the ways and with the wariness that characterize the methods of more traditional natural historians like Gilbert White. By insisting on the identification of true history and natural history, and by calling himself, explicitly and implicitly, a natural historian, Thoreau places himself firmly within a methodology and a literary tradition. In Thoreau's time, both the method and the genre were undergoing revision and at times outright attack by a newly professionalizing scientific community. Thoreau's hope seems to have been to maintain the old, and as it turned out dying, synthesis of literature, thought, and scientific inquiry which the naturalists represented. He sets this older, more loose and wideranging science against the new professionals; he is, he insists, no scientist but a true scientist. All science, he argues, evaporates at the Transcendental moment; yet even at the rainbow's end—or at least when, later, he tries to render an account of his moment of translation to purer air—the habits of the naturalist stay with him. The single fact will redeem man, the single moment will transform him; but in the evangelizing of the fallen, even the redemptive moment may gain from corroboration.

Thoreau's history is natural not only methodologically; it is natural also in its localism. Emerson had set a biographical model for the new Transcendental history; the result was a history of sorts (and especially of the new, reformed sort) called *Representative Men.* Thoreau's longer works bear the titles not of individuals or of mankind *in toto,* but of places—a river, a pond, a peninsula, a forest, a country. This is, in part, the result of editorial decisions made after Thoreau's death; but it is nonetheless true in an important way to the nature of the works. Thoreau can comprehend Man only by comprehending himself; and, like any naturalist, he can comprehend himself or any other being only in a place. His historical disquisitions and researches, his use of the old authorities, arise most commonly from his consideration of a place— the Concord River, for instance, or a Cape Cod town, or the city of Quebec. His histories are, in their origins at least, more geographical or topographical than biographical. Of course those histories are populated, and often quite memorably so, by the famous (Champlain, for instance) and by the nearly (or even altogether) forgotten, like Hannah Dustan in *A Week* or the Reverend Osborn and the Indian Lieutenant of Eastham. But no matter how colorful or exemplary, these figures are significant only in relation to a landscape, and in relation to Thoreau himself. Emerson established the equation of history with biography and autobiography; Thoreau adds geography to the formula but holds true to the fundamental Emersonian point. The only history of real importance is that history which the self can somehow re-experience, by walking, in an image much admired by both Emerson and Thoreau, over the ground personally. *Cape Cod* is, in part, the literary record of just such an effort—a personal excursion through history by way of the terrain.

This insistence on place—a characteristic element of the genre of natural history—is the consistent note in Thoreau's work which serves to make him the most *grounded,* the most settled and topographical of Transcendentalists. It provides too a workable method of using history as a sort of guidebook to the all-important present, to be employed skeptically, as any seasoned traveler does any guidebook. And it allows Thoreau to be true both to his love of antiquarian lore and to his firm belief that only by using all the senses to comprehend the immediate experience can one proceed in the radical and (in his case) unrelenting task of obeying the very old injunction: Know Thyself.

Thoreau's history is "natural" in another important way. The old book he cites near the beginning of *A Week* is, we recall, Johnson's *Wonder-Working Providence;* his sources for his history of Eastham are church records. These works, and others like them, which constitute the greater part of the material available in his reading of parochial history, can justly be called supernatural histories. Their point, as Johnson's title shows, is to reveal the hand of God at work in New England; they are ecclesiastical and even theological works. The interest of these historians is not this world but the Other; the most important active force is not man but the providential agency of God. Along the way, as Thoreau noticed, the historians collected a wealth of data about customs and topography; but in an important way this material, the part of the old authorities which is of interest to Thoreau, is only a by-product. Thoreau, in his commentaries, shifts the focus to the natural, the worldly, and the human. He uses the materials very selectively; and by doing so, while working with sources that are radically opposite in intention to his own work and his own beliefs, he proves, in the extreme case, that history, if properly read, can be read safely and productively.

The risk in such reading, as we have seen, is burial in a mass of useless and distorted information. This danger lies not only in history but in all of the data gathered by the world's disciplines. Thoreau was a good enough classicist to know that history is, etymologically, not a written record or a body of data, but an inquiry. The connection between his inquiry and the knowledge which is its intended result is precisely one of the questions of most concern to him. The verbal link between history and the science of natural history is not just a modern pun; taking both words, as he so often liked to do, in the most comprehensive and etymological sense possible, history (*historein,* to inquire) and science (*scio,* to know) are intimately related at their linguistic roots. That kind of interrelationship was to Thoreau, and to the Transcendentalists generally, of profound importance, concerned as they all were with the ultimate question of the source and role of language. On a more practical level, history and the records of other "sciences" are all equally troublesome, because second-hand. History carries with it the added difficulty of being almost impossible to verify experientially—one cannot, in the end, go over historical ground oneself, as one can with the data of the botanist. But any facts are dangerous, when they are someone else's. Indeed, the danger in *recorded* facts remains even if the record is one's own. We remember the fear Thoreau expressed to Harrison Blake: "I shall perhaps be enabled to speak with more precision & authority by & by,—if philosophy and sentiment are not buried under a multitude of details" (*Correspondence,* 423–424; 21 May 1856). The multitude of details threatening Thoreau is the material of his own journal.

Thoreau, the great accumulator, lived in some fear of even his own accumulations. The accounts one *renders* and the accounts one *reads* are, viewed one way, equally suspect, because both are now past. If one is, as Thoreau was, both a reader and a writer of accounts, the question of *how* to read and write productively is of great importance. It is, after all, just such a question that separates Thoreau from Alek Therien, who lives in a world of unmediated experience which Thoreau to some degree admires. But Thoreau knows himself to be a mediator; how then can he proceed?

That is the somewhat paradoxical question with which I began this study; and Thoreau provides, in an especially elaborated form, a demonstration of the two fundamental rules in its solution. The first is to use that multitude of detail which constitutes the record of man's pursuit of knowledge only on one's own, individual, even eccentric terms. Thoreau reads Johnson for topography, not spiritual solace; and clearly the lessons he learns from the parish records of Eastham are not the lessons which the recorders intended. He reads history scientifically, as a natural historian would. And he reads science Transcendentally, for the fact, not the theory. His first note on Darwin's *Voyage of the Beagle* is a good example. What catches Thoreau's eye first (and continually thereafter) is not any of the pressing theoretical questions which Darwin at least tacitly pursues, but a small anecdote about guinea fowl which can be put to immediate personal use—"I am like those guinea fowl" (*Journal*, II, 228; 6 June 1851). The new scientist looks for general conclusions; Thoreau insists it is only the single fact that will enlighten.

This kind of methodological sidestepping, this habit of never taking any discipline or account on its own terms, is only half the battle. One must also keep continually in mind the limits of applicability. A late journal entry makes reasonably explicit Thoreau's knotty relationship to the customary modes of inquiry:

> As it is important to consider Nature from the point of view of science, remembering the nomenclature and system of men, and so, if possible, go a step further in that direction, so it is equally important often to ignore or forget all that men presume they know, and take an original and unprejudiced view of Nature, letting her make what impression she will on you, as the first men, and all children and natural men still do. For your science, so called, is always more barren and mixed up with error than our sympathies are. (*Journal*, XIII, 168–169; 28 February 1860)

Thoreau's eye for the limitations of science, his awareness of those states of being where science is simply of no interest, and his readiness to see the error in any authority, scientific or historical, are always strong and always the final measure in his estimation of the usefulness of the accounts which he consults. And, as I have tried to show, this habitual wariness is a fundamental element in the method of the naturalist. It is important to remember, too, that it is *wariness*, and not, as some critics have said, something more absolutely dismissive. Even as Thoreau remarks on the barrenness and error of science, he makes science and sympathy equally important and repeats his wish to "go a little further" in the direction of the world's science.

The desire to be inclusive, eclectic, and (in intention, at least) synthetic informs all of Thoreau's work and helps to explain its apparent disorder at many points. Thoreau rejects disciplines and titles insofar as they are restrictive and absolute; he will not be a scientist by the world's standards because, even in his day, to be a scientist seemed to mean one could be nothing else. This again is a part of the appeal of the older tradition of the naturalist, which did not draw firm lines of limitation and which presented models of men who at least attempted to be scientists, philosophers, and writers at very nearly the same moment. The world's conjunction is *or*—be scientist *or* writer. Thoreau's is, repeatedly, *and*—he will, he insists, be a scholar *and* Adam, be a mystic, a Transcendentalist, *and* a natural philosopher to boot.

One can wonder, after reading the whole of Thoreau's work, how often the synthesis was effected—perhaps only in *Walden,* and perhaps not everywhere even in that book. But that should not undercut our appreciation of the grandness of the effort. Certainly the century and more since Thoreau's death has not solved or dissolved the problem. The heap of acquired knowledge is still there, and indeed larger; and the puzzle of what to do with it, and how not to be deadened by it, is still being posed, in words that Thoreau could easily adopt: "Of all the fictions, none is more bizarre than what we call history. From the vast compost of the human past, we rake together a sampling of the shards, or loose siftings of the topsoil, and come to terms with our ignorance."[1] Whether the past is shards or compost is precisely the nagging question. There are those who argue, as Richard Wright did, that "Our America is frightened of fact, of history."[2] But what nation *collects* more fact? We are, we like to believe, living always where Thoreau wanted to be, at the cutting edge of present and future; but each of our small towns has, somewhere, its collection of parochial history, the memorabilia of its own past. Even those parts of the country that have the most to fear or to regret in their own past have their Ike McCaslins paging for long hours through the very record which damns them; their men in brown coats who write, without knowing quite why, the history of the things men do. We still confront the problem with which Thoreau—and Anderson, and Hawthorne, and Faulkner, and Stein, and Williams, and others—grappled: what to do with the past, how to transmute the rubble of second-hand accounts into luminous and redemptive personal knowledge.

ABBREVIATIONS OF SOURCES

NOTES

INDEX

Abbreviations of Sources

Cape Cod   *Cape Cod and Miscellanies,* vol. IV of the Concord Edition of the Works of Henry David Thoreau (Boston: Houghton Mifflin, 1906)

Correspondence   *The Correspondence of Henry David Thoreau,* ed. Walter Harding and Carl Bode (Baltimore: Johns Hopkins University Press, 1970); citations include page number and date of the letter

Dial   *The Dial: A Magazine for Literature, Philosophy, and Religion,* 4 vols. (New York: Russell and Russell, 1961); citations include volume and page number

Early Essays   *Early Essays and Miscellanies,* ed. Joseph J. Moldenhauer and Edwin Moser, with Alexander Kern (Princeton: Princeton University Press, 1975)

Excursions   *Excursions and Poems,* vol. V of the Walden Edition of the Works of Henry David Thoreau (Boston: Houghton Mifflin, 1906)

"Fruits"   "Notes on Fruits," unpublished manuscript material in the Berg Collection of the New York Public Library. Although the pagination of the manuscript is incomplete and often misleading, I have included page numbers.

"Huckleberries"   "Huckleberries," in Henry David Thoreau, *The Natural History Essays,* ed. Robert Sattelmeyer (Salt Lake City: Peregrine Smith, 1980). This is an exact and more widely available reprinting of Leo Stoller's reconstruction of this essay, first published in 1970 by the University of Iowa and the New York Public Library.

Journal   *Journal,* ed. Bradford Torrey and Francis H. Allen, 14 vols. (Boston: Houghton Mifflin, 1906); citations include volume, page number, and date of entry

Maine Woods   *The Maine Woods,* ed. Joseph J. Moldenhauer (Princeton: Princeton University Press, 1972)

"Seeds"   "Dispersion of Seeds," unpublished manuscript in the Berg Collection of the New York Public Library. The pagination of this material, while still misleading, is much more reliable than that of "Notes on Fruits."

Walden   *Walden,* ed. J. L. Shanley (Princeton: Princeton University Press, 1973)

Week   *A Week on the Concord and Merrimack Rivers,* ed. Carl F. Hovde, William L. Howarth, and Elizabeth Hall Witherell (Princeton: Princeton University Press, 1980)

NOTES

INTRODUCTION

1. Sherwood Anderson, *The Triumph of the Egg* (New York: W. Huebsch, 1921), pp. 97-101. Because the piece is so short, I have not thought it necessary to give page references in the text. The problem of what to call the piece is suggested by Anderson himself, who variously refers to the parts of the book as "impressions" and "tales" in an explanatory subtitle.

2. R. W. B. Lewis, *The American Adam* (Chicago: University of Chicago Press, 1958); Richard Hofstadter, *Anti-Intellectualism in American Life* (New York: Knopf, 1963).

3. David Scofield Wilson, *In the Presence of Nature* (Amherst: University of Massachusetts Press, 1978), p. 34.

4. Hofstadter, *Anti-Intellectualism*, pp. 25-26. Of this as of so much else, Tocqueville seems to have been the first observer; see *Democracy in America*, vol. II, bk. 1, chap. 10.

5. Lewis, *American Adam*, p. 1.

6. Ibid., p. 6.

7. Hawthorne's lament is in the preface to *The Marble Faun;* James expands the complaint into a major argument of his *Hawthorne.* In light of my comment just below on Norman Foerster, it is worth noting that James quite clearly makes the argument that since we have no history, we turn to nature.

8. William H. Gass, *In the Heart of the Heart of the Country and Other Stories* (New York: Pocket Books, 1977), p. 10.

9. I have made no effort to disguise my indebtedness to Lewis's book. But I wonder if perhaps the real American myth is that of Satan rather than Adam. America is of course not an utterly new culture, but rather a collection of transplantations. We will observe Thoreau's willingness to identify himself with the Miltonic Lucifer, and this is not, I suggest, wholly icono-

clasm or eccentricity on his part. It is intriguing to think of the number of American heroes who have a past they consider deserving of denial, suppression, or escape: Huck, Jay Gatsby, Wing Biddlebaum, Thomas Sutpen — even Christopher Newman, whom Lewis takes, on name alone, as a latter-day Adam, but who is particularly enigmatic about some of the events of his past. The case is even clearer in the world of popular literature and film, inhabited by Rhett Butler, Shane, and Bogart's Rick. And it is present, I think, in Williams' *Paterson*, which begins with a confused and disoriented giant awakening to discover the falls (the Fall?) in New Jersey.

10. Norman Foerster, *Nature in American Literature* (New York: Macmillan, 1923), p. xi.

11. John Paul Pritchard, *Criticism in America* (Norman, Oklahoma: University of Oklahoma Press, 1956), pp. 218–221.

12. James L. Machor, "Tradition, Holism, and the Dilemmas of American Literary Studies," *Texas Studies in Literature and Language*, 22, no. 1 (Spring 1980), p. 118.

13. That range has been conclusively documented by John Aldrich Christie, *Thoreau as World Traveller* (New York: Columbia University Press and the American Geographical Society, 1965).

14. Sherman Paul, *The Shores of America: Thoreau's Inward Exploration* (Urbana: University of Illinois Press, 1972); William Howarth, *The Book of Concord* (New York: Viking Press, 1982).

I. PRESENTING THE PAST

1. A useful summary of this critical trend, tracing its beginning to Sherman Paul's *Shores of America,* is Jaime Hutchinson, " 'The Lapse of the Current': Thoreau's Historical Vision in *A Week on the Concord and Merrimack Rivers,*" *ESQ,* 25, no. 4 (4th Quarter 1979), p. 211.

2. Sherman Paul, *The Shores of America* (Urbana: University of Illinois Press, 1972), p. 111.

3. Ibid., p. 314.

4. Henry Seidel Canby, *Thoreau* (Boston: Houghton Mifflin, 1939), pp. 270–279.

5. Lawrence Buell, *Literary Transcendentalism: Style and Vision in the American Renaissance* (Ithaca: Cornell University Press, 1973), pp. 207–220.

6. I am speaking of the book as a whole, since it is clear that some parts of it were recorded, in journal fashion, at the time of the voyage. The Historical Introduction to the Princeton Edition of *A Week* summarizes the stages in the transformation of the book from jottings to an abortive essay to final form, which Thoreau identifies as one of the tasks he worked on at Walden Pond (*Week,* 433–470; *Walden,* 19–20).

7. Buell, *Literary Transcendentalism,* p. 211.

8. I verge here, as elsewhere, on the complex matter of Transcendental language theory, a subject much too large to deal with adequately in this study, least of all in a footnote. I acknowledge, however, that to distinguish word from fact as I have done here violates the important message of Emerson's *Nature:* that word and thing, word and fact, must be identical. I assume Thoreau agreed, on the whole; but I also assume that he knew that, in common practice, the identity is more dreamed of than accomplished.

9. Kevin Van Anglen has elaborated this pursuit of the Edenic in Thoreau's "Wild Apples" and reaches a somewhat more optimistic conclusion than I have. See his article "A Paradise Regained: Thoreau's *Wild Apples* and the Myth of the American Adam," *ESQ,* 27, no. 1 (1st Quarter 1981), pp. 28–37.

10. Ralph Waldo Emerson, "History" in *Essays: First Series,* ed. Joseph Slater, A. R. Ferguson, and J. F. Carr, vol. II of *The Collected Works of Ralph Waldo Emerson* (Cambridge: Harvard University Press, 1979), pp. 6–7.

11. Emerson, "History," pp. 5–6.

12. Ibid., p. 4.

13. Ibid., p. 9.

14. Stanley Cavell, *The Senses of Walden* (New York: Viking, 1973), p. 3.

15. One could, I believe, assemble a modest study to be entitled "Emblematic Scows" and evaluating Thoreau's use of this historical boat and the one earlier in *A Week* which he makes into a convincing type of the artwork, "a mixture of labor and art" (*Week,* 15–16).

16. Quoted in Michel Foucault, *The Order of Things* (New York: Random House, 1973), p. 161. Foucault's entire chapter on the origins of natural history is of great relevance (pp. 125–165), and especially his treatment of the process by which history becomes "natural" and the way in which natural history emphasizes the "almost exclusive privilege of sight" (pp. 125–138).

17. Canby, *Thoreau,* p. 327.

18. William Wordsworth, *The Prelude,* ed. Ernest de Selincourt (Oxford: Oxford University Press, 1926), bk. xii, l. 91 (of the 1850 version).

19. Ibid., bk. xiv, ll. 70 and 75–76.

20. Emerson, "History," p. 22.

2. CIRCUMSTANCES LAID TOGETHER

1. David E. Allen, *The Naturalist in Britain* (London: Allen Lane, 1976), p. 2.

2. Henry Seidel Canby, *Thoreau* (Boston: Houghton Mifflin, 1939), pp. 335–336.

3. Charles Darwin, *The Voyage of the Beagle,* ed. Leonard Engel (Garden City, N.Y.: Doubleday, 1962), p. xxi. All further references to this work are identified in the text, using the short title *Beagle* followed by the page number.

4. The issue of the proper title to assign Darwin during his time on the *Beagle* serves to emphasize the absence of strict professional categories at the time. Stephen Jay Gould summarizes the recent assertion that to call Darwin "the naturalist of the *Beagle*" is, strictly speaking, an error. See his *Ever Since Darwin: Reflections in Natural History* (New York: Norton, 1979), pp. 28–33.

5. Darwin's biographer, Sir Gavin de Beer, underscores the point being made here by using the same image of the self-trained schoolboy to describe Darwin when he went aboard the *Beagle.* See his *Charles Darwin: Evolution by Natural Selection* (Garden City, N.Y.: Doubleday, 1964), p. 38.

6. Other, and more American instances, can be found in the lives of Alexander Wilson and Audubon. See Joseph Kastner, *A Species of Eternity* (New York: Knopf, 1977), pp. 163 and 206. The only real path of "professional" scientific training in the early part of the century—the path followed by both Asa Gray and Louis Agassiz—was that of medicine. See A. Hunter Dupree, *Asa Gray* (Cambridge: Harvard University Press, 1959), p. 33; and Edward Lurie, *Louis Agassiz: A Life in Science* (Chicago: University of Chicago Press, 1960), pp. 41–58.

7. I base this estimate on Edward A. Martin, *A Bibliography of Gilbert White* (London: Halton and Company, 1934), pp. 90–139. Thoreau's personal copy of *NHS* is listed in Walter Harding, *Thoreau's Library* (Charlottesville, Va.: University of Virginia Press, 1957), p. 98. That edition, published in London in 1854, did not (apropos of a point made later in the chapter) contain either the *Antiquities* or White's "Advertisement" to the first edition.

8. Canby, *Thoreau,* p. 365.

9. Ibid., p. 433. The presumed similarity between the two men has had a more recent elaboration, from a rather different perspective, in W. H. Auden's "Posthumous Letter to Gilbert White," *Collected Poems,* edited by Edward Mendelson (New York: Random House, 1976), pp. 667–668. Oddly enough, the poem seems to continue the misreading of Thoreau inherent in the comments of his contemporaries. Auden proposes the idea that Thoreau "might well have/found in you the Ideal Friend he wrote of/with such gusto." It is a point so speculative as not to be susceptible of useful discussion; but the notion that (in Auden's phrase) "the quietest of curates" would have satisfied the eccentric, even perverse standards of friendship laid out in *A Week* seems to me impossible.

10. Ralph Waldo Emerson, introductory note to "The Natural History

of Massachusetts," *Dial,* III, 19.

11. The letter to Duyckinck is quoted in *Thoreau: Man of Concord,* ed. Walter Harding (New York: Holt, Rinehart and Winston, 1960), p. 176. Hawthorne's brief account of his first impression of Thoreau when they met in 1842 — an account which serves to mitigate somewhat the harshness of Hawthorne's comments to Duyckinck — can be found in *The American Notebooks,* ed. Claude M. Simpson (Columbus: Ohio State University Press, 1972), pp. 353–357.

12. This and all further references to White's book are taken from *The Natural History of Selborne* (New York: Penguin Books, 1977), a recent and readily available text. Aside from modernization of punctuation and spelling, it does not differ from the earlier editions I have consulted, including the 1854 edition which Thoreau owned. The problem of citation, given the bewildering variety and number of editions, is a difficult one; I have adopted the (I hope) useful practice of identifying all quotations in the text using the abbreviation *NHS* followed by the *date* of the letter. Since none of the letters is more than a few pages long, this should allow ease of reference to the widest possible number of editions.

13. Allen, *Naturalist in Britain,* pp. 20–25; his remarks on White's disingenuousness are on page 22.

14. One wonders if the marked change in the nature and form of White's letters when he changes correspondents is a reason for his choice, in the first edition of *Selborne,* not to organize the book strictly by chronology. The arrangement certainly makes the pattern I am describing more clear, although a number of White's editors have preferred a chronological arrangement.

15. Actually, he uses two systems. Letters I and II are both arranged by time of arrival of the respective species; Letter II is further arranged on the basis of bird-song types.

16. *NHS,* 11/20/1773, on house-martins; *NHS,* 1/29/1774, on chimney swallows; and *NHS,* 9/28/1774, on swifts are the clearest examples.

17. *NHS,* 10/29/1770, discusses the evils of relying on memory rather than observation; and *NHS,* 6/30/1769, emphasizes the necessity of observing the actual subject rather than relying on written accounts.

18. The letters are, among other things, the only ones not dated; see Martin, *Bibliography of Gilbert White,* p. 30.

19. Allen, *Naturalist in Britain,* p. 2.

20. See *NHS,* 2/7/1776; *NHS,* 4/29/1776; and *NHS,* 1/8/1778.

21. See *NHS,* 5/21/1770, and *NHS,* 12/9/1773.

22. He is not always so gentle in his treatment of superstition; see *NHS,* 7/27/1768, and *NHS,* 1/8/1776.

23. Martin, *Bibliography of Gilbert White,* lists only five editions up to 1854 which include the *Antiquities.*

24. Thoreau's first *Journal* entry concerning White dates from March 1853; this would suggest he read White before purchasing his own copy, dated 1854. My investigation of the standard sources on Thoreau's reading, and an inquiry directed to the staff of the Princeton Edition, have produced no indication that Thoreau read White before 1853. It would be tempting, considering Emerson's great fondness for White (see his *Journals and Miscellaneous Notebooks,* ed. W. H. Gilman et al. [Cambridge: Harvard University Press, 1960–1978], vol. X, pp. 166–167), to imagine Thoreau finding a copy of White in Emerson's library during his time as a member of the Emerson household. However, if Walter Harding's *Emerson's Library* (Charlottesville, Va.: University of Virginia Press, 1967) is a conclusive list, Emerson did not own a copy of the book.

25. *Journal,* II, 228 (6 June 1851); 240–248 (11 June 1851); and 261–264 (14 June 1851). J. A. Christie, *Thoreau as World Traveller* (New York: Columbia University Press and the American Geographical Society, 1965) makes frequent reference to Thoreau's reliance on Darwin; see especially pp. 74–81.

26. *Journal,* V, 65 (29 March 1853) and 83 (2 April 1853); VII, 449 (2 August 1855); and XII, 156–157 (23 April 1859). The last entry is on the subject of earthworms (both White and Darwin are, in certain circles, famous for their interest in these worms), which is also the subject of one of Emerson's entries on White (*Journals and Notebooks,* vol. II, p. 326).

27. Allen, *Naturalist in Britain,* p. 176. Jacques Barzun objects to this description, which is a commonplace one and by no means original to Allen. Barzun finds Darwin "pre-eminently an observer and recorder of facts" — intended as damnation by faint praise. See *Darwin, Marx, Wagner* (Boston: Little Brown, 1941), p. 80.

28. Allen, *Naturalist in Britain,* chap. 4. Allen comments (p. 83), on the issue of professionalism in the early nineteenth century, that the "almost total absence of a separate world of professional science was one way in which the first half of the Victorian age differed quite sharply from the second."

29. See de Beer, *Charles Darwin,* pp. 24–31; and Darwin's *Autobiography,* lately published along with that of T. H. Huxley in an edition prepared by de Beer (London: Oxford University Press, 1974). Pages 8–12 and 22–40 of the *Autobiography* are particularly relevant. As partial evidence of Darwin's interest in the "profession" of science, witness the statement in the *Autobiography* (p. 40) that, on the eve of the voyage, even after his association with Henslow was well established, "I would have thought myself mad to give up the first days of partridge-shooting for geology or any other science." This should be discounted, somewhat, in

view of Darwin's effort to present himself throughout the *Autobiography* as being, when young, a typical idler of the huntin'-and-shootin' sort.

30. Darwin, *Autobiography,* p. 39.

31. Darwin calls this an account. I might remark here on what may be obvious: the frequency with which all these writers use the word *account.* Thoreau's use of the term in *Walden,* which is of course an important word-play expressive of his particular slant on "economics," is at the same time a customary and even rather tired usage—the accepted name for the somewhat undefined sort of writing in which he engages in *Walden* and elsewhere.

32. Darwin edits the lines, slightly and silently, by placing a full stop after "doubt." Shelley's text continues, with only a comma after "doubt":

> or faith so mild,
> So solemn, so serene, that men may be,
> In such a faith, with nature reconciled . . .

See Shelley, *Poetical Works,* ed. Thomas Hutchinson, with corrections by G. M. Matthews (London: Oxford University Press, 1970) p. 533, ll. 77–79. The alteration is indicative of the degree to which Darwin, while influenced by the prevailing intellectual winds of Romanticism in his youth, is in the end not a Romantic. The idea of a reconciling faith arising from nature is not to his taste.

33. The skill with which Darwin here manages to familiarize the (potentially) terrific is even more apparent when this passage is compared to the same scene as described in the opening paragraphs of the first sketch in Melville's "The Encantadas." Another striking example of this domestication of the marvelous in Darwin occurs when he explains the action of earthquakes—which he acknowledges to be among the most awe-inspiring of his experiences—by using the analogy of a piece of paper and a handful of pins. The analogy is precise and elucidating; and at the same time it reduces the most destructive of natural forces to the serenely domestic level of a Victorian parlor. See *Beagle,* 310–311.

34. He is even remarkably fair in speaking of those invariably troublesome creatures, missionaries (*Beagle,* 423–424).

35. See de Beer, *Charles Darwin,* chaps. 2 and 3.

36. The passage from Darwin is from *Beagle,* 4.

37. Perry Miller, *Consciousness in Concord* (Boston: Houghton Mifflin, 1958), pp. 12–27 and 109–116; J. Lyndon Shanley, *The Making of Walden* (Chicago: University of Chicago Press, 1957), pp. 19–23.

38. Miller, *Consciousness in Concord,* p. 109.

3. THE GENRE OF NATURAL HISTORY

1. William Ellery Channing, *Thoreau the Poet Naturalist,* ed. F. B. Sanborn (Boston: Charles E. Goodspeed, 1902). See especially page 61 on Tho-

reau's "study of old writers on Natural History" and Thoreau's rejection of "recent scientific pate-de-fois-gras"; and page 67 for Channing's estimation of Thoreau as scientist and as naturalist.

2. Walter Harding and Michael Meyer, *The New Thoreau Handbook* (New York: New York University Press, 1980), p. 69. The publication and subsequent revision of Carl Bode's *Collected Poems of Henry Thoreau* (Baltimore: Johns Hopkins University Press, rev. ed. 1970) provoked serious reconsideration of Thoreau's verse. *The New Thoreau Handbook* lists (p. 88) the important articles, most of them written since 1970.

3. Channing, especially on the pages cited in note 1 above, takes this "charge" and makes it a commendation.

4. James Russell Lowell, "Thoreau," in *The Writings of James Russell Lowell* (Boston, 1892), vol. I pp. 361–381. The quoted comments come from pp. 368–370. The essay as a whole, while in its way a defense of Thoreau, is also intensely critical, often on surprising grounds—for instance, that "Thoreau had no humor" (p. 374). Lowell may, when he wrote the essay, still have had in mind his disagreement with Thoreau over Lowell's emendation of Thoreau's material in *The Atlantic Monthly*—at which point Thoreau's sense of humor was, to be sure, little in evidence (*Correspondence,* 515–516; 22 June 1858).

5. John Burroughs, "Henry D. Thoreau," in *Indoor Studies,* vol. VIII of the Riverby Edition of *The Writings of John Burroughs* (Boston: Houghton Mifflin, 1904), pp. 38–39.

6. See Burroughs, "Henry D. Thoreau," pp. 39–40; and "Another Word on Thoreau," in *The Last Harvest* (Boston: Houghton Mifflin, 1922), pp. 135–138.

7. Burroughs, "Henry D. Thoreau," p. 38.

8. Ibid., p. 41.

9. See Harding and Meyer, *New Thoreau Handbook,* pp. 58–60 and the bibliography on pp. 153–154. Robert Sattelmeyer's introduction to Thoreau's *Natural History Essays* (Salt Lake City: Peregrine Smith, 1980) is a more elaborate defense, which however shies away from any final claims for the purely scientific value of Thoreau's work. The standard article on Thoreau and science remains Nina Baym's "Thoreau's View of Science," *Journal of the History of Ideas,* 26 (April-June 1965), pp. 221–234. The article seems to me to make Thoreau's ultimate convictions on the value of science rather more clear-cut and hostile than is warranted; and it fails to take into full account Thoreau's ongoing use of the methods of science even while he expresses doubts about the claims made by scientists as to the final value of science as a world-view.

10. One example can be seen in Burroughs' treatment of Gilbert White as opposed to his more critical remarks on Thoreau's confusion over the

identity of the ovenbird. See "The Literary Treatment of Natural History" in Burroughs' *Literary Values,* vol. X of the Riverby Edition (Boston: Houghton Mifflin, 1904), pp. 189–196; and "Another Word on Thoreau," p. 136.

11. Burroughs, "Another Word on Thoreau," p. 120.

12. The continuance of the mode is documented in the popular study by Paul Brooks, *Speaking for Nature* (Boston: Houghton Mifflin, 1981).

13. I have here dealt rather quickly with two questions that have attracted some scholarly attention. The correct dating of the "golden age of natural history" is considered in William Smallwood, *Natural History and the American Mind* (New York: Columbia University Press, 1941), p. 215 and pp. 337–353; in Philip Hicks, *The Development of the Natural History Essay in American Literature* (Philadelphia: University of Pennsylvania Press, 1924), pp. 39–62; Joseph Kastner, *A Species of Eternity* (New York: Knopf, 1977); and in the first chapter of David S. Wilson, *In the Presence of Nature* (Amherst: University of Massachusetts Press, 1978). The problem of what to call these writers is another sticky point. I have adopted the conservative position of calling them what they seem most often to have called themselves, *natural historians,* realizing that this makes no distinction between science, methodology, and literary genre, each of which seems to have some independent existence. David Wilson has attempted to devise a new name—"nature reporter"—but his reasons for using the term are to me unconvincing. Wilson is, however, to be commended for his effort to treat his subjects as writers and to restore to view an active culture of natural history investigation in eighteenth-century America.

14. Richard Lebeaux, in *Young Man Thoreau* (New York: Harper, 1978), using evidence culled from Walter Harding's *The Days of Henry David Thoreau* (New York: Knopf, 1965), suggests another and nonliterary reason for Thoreau's turn to naturalism. It may be, as Harding (p. 10) and Lebeaux (p. 58) argue, that John Thoreau the younger was, during his brother's youth, the better naturalist of the two. But if John introduced, either intentionally or by example, his young brother to the serious study of nature, Henry progressed rapidly enough to undertake the teaching of all scientific subjects in the brothers' school in 1838–1841 (Harding, pp. 81–82). There seems, therefore, to be little need to assume that Thoreau turned to natural history to pay off some psychological debt to his tragically dead brother.

15. Warner Berthoff, *A Literature Without Qualities* (Berkeley: University of California Press, 1979), pp. 31–32.

16. The question of the genres into which the writing of American Transcendentalists can be said to fall is a major subject of Lawrence Buell's *Literary Transcendentalism* (Ithaca: Cornell University Press, 1973).

17. *The Poetry of Earth,* ed. E. D. H. Johnson (New York: Atheneum,

1966), p. vii. Johnson's brief introductory explanation of the characteristics of natural history writing is invaluable.

18. Max Meisel, *A Bibliography of American Natural History: The Pioneer Century* (Brooklyn: Premier Publishing Company, 3 vols. 1924–1929). Volume I contains the bibliography of published material. One is tempted to dismiss much of it as trivial, since so many titles constitute the reports of exploratory expeditions — until one recalls that Darwin's *Voyage of the Beagle* is just such a report.

19. Hicks, *Development of the Natural History Essay*, p. 6.

20. Ibid., pp. 23–29 (on Bartram), 29–30 (on moralized nature), and 30–39 (on Crevecoeur).

21. Smallwood, *Natural History and the American Mind*, pp. 217–228 on children's books; pp. 30–41 and 86–99 on travel and correspondence.

22. Quoted in ibid., p. 3.

23. Johnson, *Poetry of Earth*, p. ix.

24. Ibid., p. xii. David Wilson, in one of his more challenging arguments, insists that the role of the American naturalist was necessarily subversive — more, that is, than merely ill-at-ease within the prevailing culture. See his *In the Presence of Nature*, pp. 13–14.

25. Johnson, *Poetry of Earth*, p. xiii.

26. Kastner, *Species of Eternity*, p. 172.

27. Burroughs, "Science and Literature," in *Indoor Studies*, p. 49. There are of course natural histories which adopt a more abstract form and undertake a more abstract argument. A notable (not to say infamous) example, well known as a textbook to Thoreau, is William Smellie's *The Philosophy of Natural History*, which countless students, at Harvard and elsewhere, had to memorize. First published in its most widely used form (as edited and revised by John Ware) in Halifax, Nova Scotia, in 1824, it reached a sixth edition by 1844, one that I was able to consult. The book relentlessly works from general to particular and observes only to buttress generalization; it is basically an extended defense of the Great Chain of Being. It is radically different from the kinds of works being considered in this study, and yet it is avowedly a work of natural history, and a dismally influential one at that — serving, perhaps, as a cautionary example of how ill-defined this genre is.

28. Johnson, *Poetry of Earth*, p. xv.

29. John Muir seems to have been one. See H. F. Smith, *John Muir* (New York: Twayne, 1965), especially pp. 133–135. On the origins of natural history writing among the *virtuosi* or polymath laymen of the eighteenth century, see Kastner, *Species of Eternity*, p. 5.

30. I undertake these national distinctions only very tentatively. The ease with which the example of Howitt may be applied to Thoreau, and the relatively close fit between Johnson's descriptions of English naturalists and

the work of Thoreau and other American writers suggest a great deal of transatlantic commonality.

31. For Buffon, see Smallwood, *Natural History and the American Mind,* pp. 124–8, and Kastner, *Species of Eternity,* pp. 122–123. The most formidable and well-known American rebuttal is of course Jefferson's *Notes on Virginia.*

32. Kastner, *Species of Eternity,* p. 153, recounts the entertaining, if less literary, example of Charles Wilson Peale's national museum. Wilson, *In the Presence of Nature,* p. 35, argues that "protonational enthusiasm" was a consistent motivating force behind the work of eighteenth-century American naturalists.

33. Hicks, *Development of the Natural History Essay,* pp. 9–10.

34. *The Travels of William Bartram,* ed. Frances Harper (New Haven: Yale University Press, 1958), p. li.

35. Hicks, *Development of the Natural History Essay,* p. 24.

36. Ibid., p. 86, for example; a great many more examples can be found in Lowell's "Thoreau."

37. We have become so used to the idea of the arrogance of science—more often than not, in the form of the Frankenstein myth—that we must remind ourselves that it is possible to be at once humble and (occasionally) scientific. Thoreau is a nicely complex example. Part of his arrogance, we observe, is his refusal to take at face (or any other) value the assertions of objectivity and rigor which are essential to the modern scientist's self-assurance. In this regard, Nina Baym is surely right when she argues that Thoreau prefers "the old naturalists"—who are, like Gilbert White, a wholly un-Frankensteinian lot. See her "Thoreau's View of Science," p. 234.

38. Introduction to Thoreau's *Natural History Essays,* pp. xxix and xxv.

39. Norman Foerster, *Nature in American Literature* (New York: Macmillan, 1923), p. 2; see also Wilson, *In the Presence of Nature,* p. 14.

40. William Howitt, *The Book of the Seasons; or, The Calendar of Nature* (London: 4th ed., 1836), p. xiii. Further references are cited in the body of the text, using the short title *Howitt* followed by the page number.

41. At various points in "Dispersion of Seeds" Thoreau pastes in excerpts from a newspaper printing of the lecture ("Seeds," 68, 303, 306, 313). At other points he clearly cross-references the manuscript to the lecture with marginal notes (e.g. "Seeds," 244, 288, 368).

4. SCHOOLING THE EYE

1. Robert F. Sayre provides a useful brief summary of the history of the idea that Thoreau "was a romantic who peaked young"—which he then goes on to demolish—in *Thoreau and the American Indians* (Princeton: Princeton University Press, 1977), pp. 101–105.

2. This evidence has been brought to light primarily by Leo Stoller, who managed to reconstruct a working text of "Huckleberries" from the confused manuscript "Notes on Fruits"; by William Howarth's catalog of the manuscript "Nature Notes" in *The Literary Manuscripts of Henry David Thoreau* (Columbus: Ohio State University Press, 1974), pp. 306–331; and by Robert Sayre's reconsideration of the supposed "book about the Indians" which had been described as the work of Thoreau's last years.

3. Ralph Waldo Emerson, "Thoreau," in *Lectures and Biographical Sketches,* vol. X of the Centenary Edition of *The Complete Works of Ralph Waldo Emerson* (Boston: Houghton Mifflin, 1911), p. 484.

4. Sherman Paul, *Shores of America* (Urbana: University of Illinois Press, 1972), pp. 399–400; Robert F. Sayre, *Thoreau and Indians,* p. 102.

5. The most significant catalog in "Dispersion of Seeds" is of course the preparation which Thoreau made for it by culling his *Journal* and assembling charts by month, by phenomenon, and by kind (including a listing, dear to the spirit of Gilbert White, of "Birds for April &c in order of earliest arrival of each ever noticed"; Howarth, *Literary MS of HDT,* p. 311, item F19[1]). That effort to make the observations of the previous decade available in more rigorous and schematic form, may have begun as early as 1855 and was still underway as late as December 1861. Howarth, *Literary MS of HDT,* pp. 314 (item F23a), 320 (item F28a), and 327 (item F31a) establish the earlier date; pp. 314 (item F22c) and 317 (item F24c) suggest the later. Page 322 (item F28e) suggests that Thoreau was still about this work very shortly before his death.

6. See *NHS,* 11/9/1773, and above p. 29.

7. See "Seeds" 14–24v and 3r–4, 63–64, 307–311. The latter represents continuous text, despite the confusion of page numbers.

8. The number of citations is quite considerable. My own rough count finds over 40 "authorities" — including Sophia Thoreau and John Thoreau, Sr. The range is equally wide. Loudon is a favorite, and familiar to readers of "The Succession of Forest Trees." Darwin is there as well — and this time Thoreau includes *Origin of Species.* Thoreau cites White's correspondent Thomas Pennant, although not Gilbert White himself. The references stretch chronologically from Homer, Virgil, Pliny, Theophrastus, and Herodotus to "a correspondent of the Tribune" in 1861; and include along the way George B. Emerson, Michaux, Alexander Wilson, Evelyn, Bartram, and Linnaeus.

9. The warning can be found in both the Old and the New Testaments — Isaiah XI:6 and Peter I:24.

10. I have, perhaps arbitrarily, excluded "Walking." It is recognizably less an essay on natural history than those which I have included, although I believe the same habits of mind could be discovered there. And it is less

distinctly a work of the end of Thoreau's life. Howarth's *Literary MS of HDT* records drafts of the lecture from as early as 1851 (pp. 145–149), although Thoreau was in 1857 unwilling to see it printed as yet, and submitted it for publication only in March of 1862 (*Correspondence*, 477–478, 26 April 1857; and p. 640, 11 March 1862).

11. See Robert F. Stowell, *A Thoreau Gazetteer*, ed. William L. Howarth (Princeton: Princeton University Press, 1970), p. 32.

12. The catalog of the good and the bad is scattered throughout the essay, and includes many familiar figures—the mower (*Excursions*, 253), the farmer (p. 256), tithing-men and Puritans (p. 262), and drovers (p. 266) are clearly among the lost. The peculiar triad of more elevated spirits can be found on p. 308 of *Excursions* and should of course be enlarged by one to include Indians (p. 258).

13. One could be pedantic and insist that the "I" which begins Stoller's version of "Huckleberries" is not Thoreau but Virgil.

14. It is difficult as things now stand to determine where "Dispersion of Seeds" would, in final form, have begun; but a considerable diminution of the eccentricity of the "I" of that work is indicated by the fact that Thoreau did not carry over into "Dispersion" in its present form the introductory pages of "The Succession of Forest Trees" (*Excursions*, 184–186). He thus omitted a prolonged exposition of his own "oddity."

A Week on the Concord and Merrimack Rivers does not demonstrate this shift of style so markedly; "I" is noticeably missing from the opening section, "Concord River," and the beginning of the excursion itself is dominated by "we." That we, however, is clearly personal—"we two, brothers" (*Week*, 15)—and does not suggest a bond between Thoreau and his reader. My observations on pronouns may in the end be a sidetrack, although I think they help explain the distinct difference in mood and effect between Thoreau's earlier works and most of these late essays. In any case, final resolution of the matter will await the efforts of someone with more patience—or more access to word-processing equipment—than I, who can follow the "I" throughout these essays.

15. A similar, if not exactly parallel, movement can be found in "Huckleberries," 215–217, where Thoreau begins by picking the berries himself ("I pluck a handful from one bush") only to be replaced by "you" who "gather some" and who will "tomorrow" go even further, to a point where "you" find yourself so surrounded by berries that "you seem to have travelled into a foreign country, or else are dreaming."

16. Lewis Thomas, *The Lives of a Cell* (New York: Viking, 1974).

17. John Burroughs, "Science and Literature" and "Science and the Poets," in *Indoor Studies* (Boston: Houghton Mifflin, 1904); "The Literary Treatment of Natural History" in *Literary Values* (Boston: Houghton

Mifflin, 1904); "The Naturalist's View of Life" in *The Breath of Life* (Boston: Houghton Mifflin, 1915); and "Literature and Science" in *Under the Apple-Trees* (Boston: Houghton Mifflin, 1916). His essays on Gilbert White are also relevant: "Gilbert White's Book" in *Indoor Studies* and "Gilbert White Again" in *Literary Values*.

18. Precisely when the split occurs is another probably irresolvable question in the history of natural history. See Philip Hicks, *The Development of the Natural History Essay in American Literature* (Philadelphia: University of Pennsylvania Press, 1924), pp. 61–62; William Smallwood, *Natural History and the American Mind* (New York: Columbia University Press, 1941), pp. 145, 162, and 239–248; and Joseph Kastner, *A Species of Eternity* (New York: Knopf, 1977), p. 284, for informed considerations of the issue.

19. This generalization demands immediate qualification. There have been since Thoreau's day "serious" amateur scientist/writers—notably John Muir. The development in this century of the new "science" of ecology encouraged a period of serious amateur study, although that science now has developed its own sense of credentials, which will almost inevitably wither amateurism.

20. To attack the problem from that angle one could profitably study the lives of Louis Agassiz and Asa Gray, the men most responsible for the professionalization of American science and scientific training. Agassiz, as a youth, decided to be a "man of letters," and did not, apparently, ever renounce that aim. And he may be said to have kept the amateurs in business, if only as field collectors (among whom we find Thoreau himself). But clearly such collectors were at most the handmaidens of science. See Edward Lurie, *Louis Agassiz: A Life of Science* (Chicago: University of Chicago Press, 1960) and A. Hunter Dupree, *Asa Gray* (Cambridge: Harvard University Press, 1959).

5. NATURALIZING EDEN

1. Sherman Paul, *The Shores of America* (Urbana: University of Illinois Press, 1972), p. 396.

2. Ibid., p. 396.

3. Ibid., p. 275; see also p. 105 for Thoreau's preference for "sympathy" over "scientific method" in "The Natural History of Massachusetts."

4. Ibid., p. 275, provides a summary of these entries.

5. Thoreau omits reading as a skill of the scientist: "Would you be a reader, a student merely, or a seer?" (*Walden,* 111)

6. Michel Foucault, *The Order of Things* (New York: Random House, 1973), pp. 130–131 and 157–161.

7. See J. L. Shanley, *The Making of Walden* (Chicago: University of Chicago Press, 1957), pp. 30–33.

8. See *Walden,* 15, 25, 57, 63, 88, 91, 131, and 164. The similarities—and differences—between this kind of "sainthood" and a more traditional Protestant variety, may be seen by considering the experience recounted in Jonathan Edwards' "Personal Narrative" and Edwards' description of "evangelical humiliation" as a necessary accompaniment of "gracious affections" in his *Treatise Concerning Religious Affections,* ed. J. E. Smith (New Haven: Yale University Press, 1959), p. 311.

9. Perry Miller, *Consciousness in Concord* (Boston: Houghton Mifflin, 1958), pp. 51–52.

10. Ibid., p. 34.

11. Paul, *Shores of America,* pp. 10–16 and 49–57.

12. Here as elsewhere, the (perhaps accidental(analogies between Thoreau and more traditional naturalists are striking. Joseph Kastner cites a similar list of "professions" in the case of the colorful Constantine Rafinesque; see *A Species of Eternity* (New York: Knopf, 1977), p. 242. Kastner's book as a whole persuasively demonstrates the degree to which the practice of naturalism in the early nineteenth century demanded an acquaintance with a wide variety of skills and occupations. Thoreau's disguise as hydra must also be considered as a part of the tradition of the boaster as an American comic type, as Constance Rourke demonstrated some years ago in her *American Humor* (New York: Harcourt Brace, 1931). Thoreau's picture of himself as a man of many skills and no profession goes hand in hand with his interest in the early settlers of New England. He must have realized that, when Concord was born, a man who could justly claim to be a carpenter, surveyor, painter, schoolmaster, mason, and more besides would have been a prized addition to the town, not an eccentric or a ne'er-do-well.

13. Nathaniel Hawthorne, *American Notebooks,* ed. Claude M. Simpson (Columbus: Ohio University Press, 1972), pp. 353–354.

14. The same point is of course developed more fully in "Economy" (*Walden,* 49–52).

15. Robert Langbaum, *The Poetry of Experience* (New York: Norton, rev. ed. 1971), p. 23.

16. The contradiction is of course intentional, as a perusal of the various comments Thoreau makes about the railroad (*Walden,* 41, 52–54, 92, 97, 114–117, and 305) or about the "virtues" of cooperation (pp. 71 and 110) would show. It is, I think, arguable that contradiction is the peculiarly American genius.

17. The elm tree also stands as a premonitory pun on the heritage of that other *Celtis occidentalis,* John Field.

18. The chapter could, on this and other grounds, bear comparison to

Hawthorne's similarly ambiguous "Custom House."

19. In exactly the same way, for instance, before measuring Walden he tells the fables of the ice-fishermen and the pickerel (*Walden*, 282–285).

20. How much this passage and the following paragraphs are literally in the style of the field naturalist can be seen clearly by a reading of Gilbert White's seventh introductory letter to *The Natural History of Selborne*, which describes ponds.

21. The layman would probably rely on some such reference as the maps included on pages 6, 8, and 9 of Robert Stowell's *A Thoreau Gazeteer*, ed. William L. Howarth (Princeton: Princeton University Press, 1970): and of course the layman would be wrong. As modern understanding of the nature and formation of glacial ponds has shown, Thoreau had his facts right. See Edward S. Deevey, Jr., "A Re-examination of Thoreau's *Walden*," *The Quarterly Review of Biology*, 17 (March 1942), pp. 1–11: and Eugene H. Walker, "Walden's Way Revealed," in *Man and Nature* (Lincoln: Massachusetts Audobon Society, 1971). I am indebted to William Howarth for correcting my own, exceedingly lay eye on this point.

22. Of course, one of the final surprises of the chapter is that Walden is not, after all, unique; there is always White's Pond if Walden fails (*Walden*, 197–200).

23. The particular document, Cellini's autobiography, is of course, in Emersonian terms, the perfect one—autobiography being the truest history.

24. This belief that the contempt and suspicion of the world are a sign of sainthood may be one reason why Thoreau takes such pleasure in *Cape Cod* in the fact that he was mistaken during his excursion for a bankrobber (*Cape Cod*, 101 and 177).

25. To the modern reader the letter takes on an unforeseen irony; that frontier paradise to which Williams had moved is Buffalo, New York.

26. See *Walden*, 29, 38, 39, and 198.

6. SUSPECTABLE REPETITIONS

1. Walter Harding, *The Days of Henry David Thoreau* (New York: Knopf, 1965), p. 361; see also Sherman Paul, *The Shores of America* (Urbana: University of Illinois Press, 1972), p. 388.

2. Other examples of "fallen" industries are the Barnstable salt works (*Cape Cod*, 27–28), the Orleans clamming business (pp. 35–36), and the oak forests of Truro (pp. 130–131).

3. The climactic importance of this vision through the knothole is emphasized by its location at the end of the final chapter of the four which Thoreau published, as a unit, in *Putnam's Magazine* in 1855.

4. The lines Thoreau quotes are lines 74–77 of the Loeb edition.

5. Osborn is Irish, as are so many of the people who interest Thoreau.

6. The connection between the Pilgrims and Eastham is direct; the town lands are first "purchased" by "the committee from Plymouth" (*Cape Cod*, 43).

7. But Emerson insists he must do so: "He should see that he can live all history in his own person." Ralph Waldo Emerson, "History," in *Essays: First Series*, ed. Joseph Slater, A. R. Ferguson, and J. F. Carr, vol. II of *The Collected Works of Ralph Waldo Emerson* (Cambridge: Harvard University Press, 1979), p. 6.

8. A modern historian might prefer Bradford's *History. Mourt's Relation* is preferable to Thoreau on two counts: as more topographical and as more familiar. Bradford's complete *History* appeared in print only in 1856, although the sections dealing with the first landings on New World soil had been available in Alexander Young's *Chronicles of the Pilgrim Fathers* (Boston, 1841)—the volume also contains *Mourt's Relation*—and in Nathaniel Morton's popular *New England's Memorial* (Boston, 1855).

9. Thoreau refers to Francis Billington, who climbed a tree and discovered a large pond on January 8, 1620 (*Cape Cod*, 256–257). It would be interesting to know whether Thoreau was at all aware of the peculiar history of the Billington name among the Pilgrims. Francis' son was lost soon after the landing and rediscovered only after considerabe anxiety and effort. John Billington was, in 1630, the colony's first murderer. Thoreau's knowledge of Bradford, where this is reported, may not have been extensive enough for him to have known about the latter case; it is not included in the text of Bradford given by either Young or Morton, although it is mentioned in a footnote in the 1855 edition of *New England's Memorial*.

CONCLUSION

1. Wright Morris, *New York Times Book Review*, 20 January 1980, p. 13. Another recent use of the same image—more elaborately and from an opposite direction—is Robert M. Adams, "Rags, Garbage, and Fantasy," in *Bad Mouth: Fugitive Essays on the Dark Side* (Berkeley: University of California Press, 1977).

2. Richard Wright, *American Hunger* (New York: Harper and Row, 1977), p. 14.

INDEX